D1578046

Be Ye Transformed

Bible Interpretation:
Acts through Revelation

by
Elizabeth Sand Turner

UNITY BOOKS
Unity Village, Missouri 64065

CONTENTS

Publisher's Note: In this book, Bible references are given in the usual way (Matt. 15:14). References with page numbers are to various Unity books, the titles of which are abbreviated as follows: ASP *(Atom-Smashing Power of Mind)*; CH *(Christian Healing)*; JCH *(Jesus Christ Heals)*; KL *(Keep a True Lent)*; MD *(Metaphysical Bible Dictionary)*; MG *(Mysteries of Genesis)*; MJ *(Mysteries of John)*; P *(Prosperity)*; RW *(The Revealing Word)*; TT *(Talks on Truth)*; TP *(The Twelve Powers of Man)*.

Unless otherwise noted, all Bible quotations are from the Revised Standard Version of the Holy Bible.

GRATEFULLY DEDICATED
to the many Unity ministers and students
whom I have had the pleasure of teaching,
and whose desire for this book prompted
its writing.

FOREWORD

Do not be conformed to this world but be you transformed by the renewal of your mind, that you may prove what is the will of God, what is good and acceptable and perfect (Rom. 12:2).

With these words Paul presents a challenge to every Christian. When one accepts Jesus Christ the task before him is to free himself from worldly standards and make the "will of God" the supreme aim of his life. To accomplish this requires a complete transformation of character, and the pertinent question asked by each individual is, "How may this transformation be brought about?" Paul answers, "By the renewal of your mind." Ignorance and inertia, resulting from lack of knowledge and the use of man's spiritual faculties, are the great obstacles for him to overcome. Yet he must do this before the "true light that enlightens every man . . . coming into the world" (John 1:9) can break through into the soul. How well this overcoming was made by the immediate followers of Jesus and how brilliant was the light that radiated from them is the theme of this book.

Be Ye Transformed is the third of a series of books on Bible interpretation based on that given by Charles Fillmore, cofounder of the Unity School of Christianity. The first, *Let There Be Light,* is on the Old Testament, and the second, *Your Hope of Glory,* is an interpretation of the life and teachings of Jesus. This book covers the early church, the ministry and epistles of Paul, the General Epistles, and The Revelation to John. All are closely related for the entire Bible is an account of man's efforts to find the God from which he came.

Jesus said, "If you know these things, blessed are you if you do them" (John 13:17). The first Christians took His words to heart and the twenty-three books of the New Testament covered in *Be Ye Transformed* relate the thrilling story of the use they made of their understanding of His teachings.

The Acts of the Apostles is a continuation of the Gospel according to Luke, and records the establishment of the first church and the spread of Christianity throughout a large part of the Greco-Roman world. It is followed by the thirteen epistles generally attributed to Paul, though some modern scholars are of the opinion that the Pastoral Epistles may have reached their final form a number of years after Paul's death. Then come the eight so-called General Epistles—Hebrews, James, First and Second Peter, First, Second, and Third John, and Jude. These were written for instruction and guidance to the then far-flung Christian churches. And lastly the Revelation, that mystical book written not only to comfort and sustain the Christian undergoing persecution by the Roman government, but to provide the true believer of all ages with a chart of his inner experiences as he walks the spiritual way laid down by Jesus Christ.

The word of God, Truth, given in all its fullness by

Jesus, was heard throughout Palestine. During the three years of His ministry a number of disciples were drawn by His teachings and healings. From among them He selected twelve who promptly left all and followed Him. The Apostles were something of a motley group, most of them fishermen belonging to the middle class of society. Yet the resurrected Jesus said to them, "You shall be my witnesses in Jerusalem and in all Judea and Samaria and to the end of the earth" (Acts 1:8). Several years later still another was called to His service and the proud Pharisee, Saul of Tarsus, became Paul the Christian missionary. What a tremendous mission was given these men! It could be accomplished only by strong souls afire with the Christ light. By them the Gospel, first preached in Jerusalem, traveled in ever-widening circles until it reached imperial Rome. Theirs was such a courageous and successful performance that it changed the course of history.

The superb teachings of Jesus Christ have enlightened and inspired us with their wisdom and power. Our utmost desire is to know them so well that we may live thereby. Surely we can do no better than to follow the example of those intrepid souls of the first century A.D., who blazed a new trail in the wilderness of mortal thinking by their understanding of and devotion to the Christ message. We too must go into our own world of thought and feeling and bear the good news of the indwelling Christ as our hope of glory.

The Apostles established not only the first but

many Christian churches. What is the church of Christ? Charles Fillmore contends that there is an inner as well as an outer church. The inner church, which is the more important, is composed of spiritual ideas in the mind of the individual that have been revealed to him by the indwelling Christ. This is the true church, so firm and strong that "the powers of death shall not prevail against it" (Matt. 16:18). It is "not made of creeds and forms, nor is it contained in walls of wood and stone; the heart of man is its temple and the Spirit of truth is the one guide into all Truth" (MD 151).

The church as an outer organization began with a group of people who had undergone a complete change in their inner life. The outpouring of the Holy Spirit at Pentecost and Paul's conversion on the Damascus road gave the Apostles the power to preach with great conviction, to heal in the name of Jesus Christ, and even to raise the dead. Those who heard them and believed also received an inward quickening. Is this possible for the modern Christian? It is what we long for. The record before us is clear. All may receive the gift of the Holy Spirit if they will open their eyes to see, their ears to hear, and their hearts to pray.

As do *Let There Be Light* and *Your Hope of Glory,* this book reminds the reader that Unity emphasizes the esoteric meaning of Scripture. As men, the characters dealt with lived in the early part of the first Christian century; as attributes of mind they dwell with us today. The Apostles and followers of Jesus signify spiritual phases of consciousness, such as Peter standing for faith, and John, love. The orthodox Jews who were in opposition to Jesus and His adherents symbolize that state of mind that is bound to the letter of the law and to the forms and ceremonies of religion. The Gentiles stand for "worldly thoughts—thoughts pertaining to the external, or thoughts that function through the senses" (MD 228). Names of countries and cities likewise have inner meanings.

When we study the Bible in this light it is easy to project ourself into the sacred narrative. Then we understand that the spiritual path we are now treading has a multitude of signposts along the way in the form of these many characters. They live in us now as constructive and destructive attitudes of mind. By a careful scrutiny of their accomplishments and failures, we may learn how to dissolve our unregenerate traits and develop our inherent spiritual faculties.

Though it is quite evident that we have not yet attained a full awareness of our unity with the indwelling Christ, Jesus encourages us to go on by giving us the final realization possible for man, "I and the Father are one" (John 10:30). Should we not proceed with faith and joy? We need only follow the One who said, "I am the way, and the truth, and the life" (John 14:6). This those valiant champions of the Christ message, the Apostles, help us to do.

Elizabeth Sand Turner

Power from On High

Acts 1-5

As the time drew near for the Feast of Pentecost in the year 29, or perhaps 30 A.D., the majority of Jerusalem's inhabitants were busily engaged in making suitable preparations for the festival. Pentecost occurred fifty days after the Passover and at the end of the spring reaping season. It lasted only one day, but what a day! The Temple would be filled with worshipers. Pentecost commemorated the giving of the Law to Moses on Mount Sinai, and Jews from all over Palestine and the vast Mediterranean area flocked to the Holy City to offer appropriate sacrifices to their God who had given them the Law for all time and who yearly gave them a harvest.

Yet within the bustling city a small group of people were not thinking of the feast near at hand but of the words spoken by the risen Lord. Jesus had said to them on one of His last appearances, "Stay in the city [Jerusalem], until you are clothed with power from on high" (Luke 24:49). Then just before the Ascension He had promised, "Before many days you shall be baptized with the Holy Spirit" (Acts 1:5). The Apostles had been inspired and awed by His ascension and it was a solemn little band of eleven who returned to Jerusalem to await the fulfillment of His promise. There they were joined by other believers increasing their number to one hundred and twenty, and even Mary, His mother, was with them. So while the many thronged the streets of Jerusalem, the followers of "the Way" (as Jesus' disciples were called until they were given the name Christians) gathered together in the upper chamber of a house in Jerusalem, probably the home of Mary, the mother of John Mark.

Peter assumed leadership of the group. This was indeed fitting, for Peter represents faith. The Apostles stand for the twelve great powers inherent in men. When led by faith these faculties are trained to function spiritually, for faith represents the first step of redemption from mortal to spiritual thought. Abraham of the Old Testament stands for faith and it was he who went forth into a new land (consciousness) at the command of the Lord. Now Peter, symbolizing a higher development of the faith faculty, was to lead man toward the new land of Christ consciousness. Peter is the chief character in the first twelve chapters of Acts. It is faith (Peter) that lays the foundation for the word of Truth (Paul, whose exploits cover the remaining sixteen chapters of the book).

As they waited in eager anticipation for the advent of the Holy Spirit, Peter proposed that someone be selected from among them to replace Judas Iscariot so that again there would be twelve Apostles. The replacement must be one who could "become with us a witness to his resurrection" (Acts 1:22). The word *witness* means to "testify to, to give evidence of; to see or know by personal experience."

He who is worthy to be an apostle is one who knows that Christ is the "resurrection and the life," one who has felt this inward vitalizing power and testifies to it.

Two worthy men were suggested, Barsabbas and Matthias. "And they prayed and said, 'Lord, who knowest the hearts of all men, show which one of these two thou hast chosen'" (Acts 1:24). They believed in Christ and did not rely on their own judgment. When faith is quickened we ask for His guidance in making any decision. "What is Thy will?" is our prayer. Under divine direction the selection of the new member was made by lots, "and the lot fell upon Matthias; and he was enrolled with the eleven apostles" (Acts 1:26). The name *Matthias* means "given wholly unto Jehovah." Judas, whose place he filled, represents the unredeemed life force in the individual expressing as selfishness and covetousness. Matthias signifies the lifting up of the life force "that it may aid the individual in laying hold of his higher, spiritual attainments" (MD 434).

At last the day of Pentecost arrived and with it the baptism of the Holy Spirit which was to endue the disciples with power from on high. The followers of Jesus were not the first nor the last to receive this spiritual baptism. The great Hebrew seers from Moses to Jesus knew of its quickening as have great Christian seers from the Apostles to Charles Fillmore, who states, "The Holy Spirit is in the world today with great power and wisdom ready to be poured out to all who look to Him for guidance" (TT 139).

What is the Holy Spirit? In Christian theology the Holy Spirit is known as the Third Person of the Trinity—Father, Son, and Holy Spirit. Charles Fillmore explains Father as God, the Supreme Being, the Absolute, Divine Mind, the source and origin of all life. Son is the Word, Christ, I AM, the divine spirit in man. Holy Spirit is the Comforter, the Spirit of Truth, the executive power of Father and Son. "Holy Spirit is not all of Being, nor the fullness of Christ, but an emanation, or 'breath' sent forth to do a definite work" (TT 134). The Trinity is not three separate gods but one God in three phases of expression. As the divine Creator, God is Father; as the divine Self in man, He is Son; and as spiritual life and power in activity, He is Holy Spirit. For all practical purposes the names are used interchangeably and we should not be confused by terms.

In our study of God and man we deal with several trinities, such as the threefold nature of man—Spirit, soul, and body; the threefold activity of mind—superconscious, conscious, and subconscious; and the threefold steps in manifestation—mind, idea, and expression. Perhaps the simplest way to think of the Holy Spirit is as the whole spirit of God in activity. The baptism of the Holy Spirit is the tremendous spiritual quickening bestowed upon those who have prepared themselves for it.

"When the day of Pentecost had come, they were all together in one place" (Acts 2:1).

The Apostles were ready to receive what had been promised them. The preparation they made is plain and can be duplicated by anyone. There are three definite steps: first, we should be at peace (remain in Jerusalem), in that calm and serene state of mind and heart which enables us to rest in the Lord. Second, our consciousness should be unified ("together"). Third, our attention is to be centered in the heaven of the mind, the upper room ("one place"), in joyful expectation. Jesus said, "If your eye is sound, your whole body will be full of light" (Matt. 6:22). As the whole consciousness is centered on God, human thought ceases and we are ready for the light from above.

> "And suddenly a sound came from heaven like the rush of a mighty wind, and it filled all the house where they were sitting. And there appeared to them tongues as of fire, distributed and rested on each one of them. And they were all filled with the Holy Spirit and began to speak in other tongues, as the Spirit gave them utterance" (Acts 2:2-4).

The gift of the Holy Spirit to the disciples at Pentecost "described the first descent into human consciousness of that dynamic substance which Jesus radiated when He raised His body vibration to the spiritual plane. This is also an individual experience, and many have testified to the powerful inrush into mind and body of this higher power."

These Bible verses describe an experience in Christ or cosmic consciousness like that of Moses at the

Burning Bush and Jesus on the Mount of Transfigu-
ration. Cosmic consciousness is a sudden and overwhelming awareness of the divine Presence with us
and entering into us, suffusing our being. It is por-
trayed here as an outpouring of power, wisdom, and
the ability to speak God's word. Power is likened to
the "rush of a mighty wind," a force that fills us and
the place where we are. Intellectually we know that
God is all power but we are not fully aware of His
power until we feel it within ourself. Then it fills
mind and body, bringing with it a sense of unlimited
vitality, zest, and an ability to accomplish far
beyond mortal capacity. Wisdom is represented by
the tongues "as of fire" which sat upon the disciples.
Wisdom enables us to understand the deep things of
God, the mystery of life. We are overwhelmingly
conscious of being one with Him and of our part in
the divine plan. Wisdom expands the mind. It scat-
ters the ignorance of mortal thought and releases an
inner light that so illumines the soul it is flooded
with divine ideas.

The result of this dynamic partaking of spiritual
life is the compulsion to speak in "other tongues."
This means to speak not in mortal consciousness, but
as God directs. Jesus said, "The word which you hear
is not mine, but the Father's who sent me" (John
14:24). He did not speak the language of mortality
but of spirituality, God's word. We have recourse to
human words only until the tongue is loosed by the
power and wisdom of God. When we receive the
baptism of the Holy Spirit, the Christ word becomes

a living and vital reality to us.

The outpouring of the Holy Spirit changes all who partake of it. Scripture attests to what it did to the Apostles. The Gospels show them as men who loved Jesus and gladly followed Him, though they were unable to understand much of His teaching. On occasions they became ambitious for power, were often discouraged, and even fearful, envious, and spiteful. The Resurrection convinced them of the validity of Jesus' words, and the times they talked with Him during the forty days between the Resurrection and the Ascension increased their understanding and faith. But they were still not strong enough spiritually to preach His message and do His works.

After Pentecost they were different men. Peter, who had denied his Lord in fear of the Jewish leaders, was to become fearless when brought before these same leaders in the Sanhedrin, the supreme court of the Jews. James and John, who had aspired to sit on the right and left hand of Jesus in His kingdom, were to forget self-interest and seek only to serve in His name. The baptism from on high completely transformed them and they preached and healed, carrying on His work so effectively that the word traveled near and far. Neither the book of Acts nor the secular history of the early church give a record of the ministry of all the Apostles, but tradition says that they scattered throughout the vast Roman Empire and established churches wherever they went.

When the disciples came from the house filled with the wonder of their great experience in the upper room, they were met by a crowd that had gathered in the streets of Jerusalem. In it were many people from different countries who had come to the Holy City for the Pentecostal feast, and they were "bewildered because that each one heard them speaking in his own language" (Acts 2:6). Some accused the disciples of being intoxicated. Peter immediately refuted this charge and launched into his first sermon. He reminded his hearers of the prophecy of Joel, that the Spirit would come upon all flesh. This prophecy had been fulfilled in Jesus and had now come upon His disciples. David, their great king, had foretold His coming but the Jews had refused to believe and had crucified the Messiah. God rebuked this blasphemy by raising Him up and it was to His resurrection that he (Peter) and his companions were witnessing.

So inspiring were Peter's words that some three thousand Jews asked what they could do to join the Christian group. "Repent, accept Jesus Christ, and be baptized" were the requirements laid down by Peter. They readily consented and this first influx of a large number of believers marks the birthday of the Christian church.

None of the disciples of Jesus separated themselves from Judaism at this time. They never even thought of doing so. They were loyal Jews who loved their religion and were convinced that Jesus was the One foretold by Hebrew prophecy. They continued to worship in the Temple and to fulfill all the obligations of Judaism. But, in addition, they had private meetings of their own. At these the Apostles instructed them, they prayed and also ate together, taking the sacrament in remembrance of Him. The Christ Spirit bound the believers into one body; they were cheerful and contented, and "they sold their possessions and goods and distributed them to all, as any had need" (Acts 2:45).

One day as Peter and John entered the Temple at the hour of prayer, a lame beggar who sat daily at the gate called Beautiful asked alms of them. Peter directed the man to look at him and John, and when he did so, Peter said:

> " 'I have no silver and gold, but I give you what I have; in the name of Jesus Christ of Nazareth, walk.' And he took him by the right hand, and raised him up; and immediately his feet and ankles were made strong. And leaping up he stood and walked and entered the temple with them, walking and leaping and praising God" (Acts 3:6-8).

This is the first recorded healing done by the Apostles in the name of Jesus Christ. The name of anything denotes the character of it: hence, the name *Jesus Christ* stands for spiritual man. The Master had promised, "Whatever you ask in my name, I will do it, that the Father may be glorified in the Son" (John 14:13). When faith (Peter) and love (John) are foremost in consciousness, we understand the lifegiving power of the inner spiritual man and affirm His wholeness.

The healing attracted the immediate attention of those in the Temple and great was their surprise and wonder. Peter took this opportunity to address them. Pointing to the one healed, Peter declared that the miracle had been performed by no power of his or John's but by their faith in the name of Jesus Christ. Again he reminded them of the tragic mistake that had been made in crucifying Him, for by His resurrection His Messiahship had been proved. Supporting himself by various prophecies from the Old Testament, Peter urged his hearers to repent and accept Jesus Christ.

Many who heard Peter were moved and believed. The scene had attracted the attention of the Sadducees who were in charge of the Temple, and they ordered the arrest of the Apostles. The Sadducees constituted the most powerful party among the Jews, though they were less numerous and also less religious than the Pharisees. Both parties represent "the religious concepts of the intellect." The Sadducees had strong materialistic beliefs and the Pharisees were "formalists, without spiritual understanding" (MD 566). Though it was the Pharisees who opposed Jesus so bitterly during the years of His ministry, it was the Sadducees who demanded His crucifixion of Pontius Pilate, the Roman procurator. The Sadducees were to be the chief persecutors of the young Christian movement from this time until Paul's imprisonment in Caesarea.

The Sadducees, unlike the Pharisees, denied the doctrine of a future life and the immortality of the soul. Therefore Peter's declaration of the resurrection of One whom they had put to death not only angered them but made them fearful. If such a teaching were to be accepted by a large number of Jews, it would lessen their authority, and what was even worse, would diminish the rich revenues they derived from the Temple.

Spiritually interpreted, these two parties represent our religious thoughts that still cling to materialism and formalism. They invariably clash with true spiritual ideas, typified by the Apostles, and attempt to silence them. We have to be staunch in our devotion to the ideas of the Christ Mind in order to free our consciousness from these false concepts.

The next day Peter and John were called before the Sanhedrin and asked by what power they had healed the lame man. Peter's answer was prompt:

> "Be it known to you all, and to all the people of Israel, that in the name of Jesus Christ of Nazareth . . . by him this man is standing before you well. This is the stone which was rejected by you builders, but which has become the head of the corner. And there is salvation in no one else, for there is no other name under heaven given among men by which we must be saved" (Acts 4:10-12).

There is only one saving power and that is Christ. We come to know Christ by following the teachings of Jesus and calling upon Him to help us. He said, "Keep my sayings," and by looking to Him we learn to do just that. Charles Fillmore states:

> "We all recognize the advantage of thought coopera-
> tion. It is much easier to hold ourselves in the true
> consciousness when we are associated with those who
> think as we do. It was the work of Jesus to establish in
> our race consciousness a spiritual center with which
> everyone might become associated mentally, regardless
> of geographical location. He said to His disciples, 'I go
> to prepare a place for you . . . that where I am, there ye
> may be also.' That place is a state of consciousness right
> here in our midst, and we can at any time connect
> ourselves with it by centering our mind upon Jesus and
> silently asking His help in our demonstrations. It is not
> the prayer of a 'worm of the dust' to a god, but of one
> who is on the way asking the guidance of one who has
> passed over the same road, and who knows all the hard
> places and how to get through them" (TT 168).

The members of the Sanhedrin were anxious that
no more preaching be done in Jesus' name and
charged the Apostles "not to speak or teach at all in
the name of Jesus. But Peter and John answered
them, 'Whether it is right in the sight of God to listen
to you rather than to God, you must judge; for we
cannot but speak of what we have seen and heard' "
(Acts 4:18-20).

Here is a big test for us. Have we the faith to stand
for what we believe to be true? We may find it com-
paratively easy to defend Truth against unbelievers
but can we defend it against our own subtle doubts?
Can we remember that there is salvation only in
Christ? Can we remember that there is always salvation in Him? When directed by faith (Peter) we can

adhere to· our spiritual conviction without fear of mortal opposition.

With further threats the Apostles were released. There was no legal charge on which to punish them and the Jewish leaders dared not antagonize the people who were, at that very moment, still praising God for the healing of the lame man.

Peter and John hastened to their fellow Christians and reported their experiences. There was great rejoicing and yet the situation presented serious aspects. Jesus had commissioned them to preach His word and now the Jewish leaders forbade them to do so. In the Second Psalm it was written, "The kings of the earth set themselves . . . against the Lord and against his Anointed" (Acts 4:26), and remembering these words the disciples prayed for resoluteness:

> " 'Lord, look upon their threats, and grant to thy servants to speak thy word with all boldness, while thou stretchest out thy hand to heal, and signs and wonders are performed through the name of thy holy servant Jesus.' And when they had prayed, the place in which they were gathered together was shaken; and they were all filled with the Holy Spirit and spoke the word of God with boldness" (Acts 4:29-31).

When we set ourself to do His will and work, we need not be deterred by outer obstructions, powerful as they may seem. God will give us the necessary courage and insure our success. Again the praying Christians were filled with the Holy Spirit and again they spoke His word boldly.

The practice of sharing "all things in common," instituted at the time the first Christians gathered as a group, had been continued. All members of the community were provided for from the money donated by those who sold their property and material possessions and put it into the general fund. At this time Barnabas, a native of Cyprus and a prominent member of the group, sold a field and laid the money at Peter's feet. His generosity inspired a couple, Ananias and Sapphira, to dispose of *some* of their holdings, but they spread the report that they were giving the entire proceeds to the church. Immediately Peter detected the deception. When one is in spiritual consciousness he is aware of any falsity.

Confronting each with dishonesty, Peter reminded them that they sinned not against man but against God. Ananias and Sapphira died suddenly and the community was awed by this example of the retribution of sin:

"There is a lurking belief in the mind that we can join the great school of spiritual development and at the same time retain our hold upon worldly thoughts. This belief represents deception. Such deception of the mind is a very subtle error and causes the would-be disciple much misery. The best way to handle it is to uncover the whole inner consciousness to Spirit and to ask to be thoroughly purified and cleansed.

"This liar and deceiver has two sides in the mind. Outwardly, or in conscious thought, it is Ananias; in the subconscious thought it appears as Sapphira. Both of these must die before the spiritual thoughts (church) will increase in numbers and in power. The best and quickest way to dissolve these errors is to face them boldly and to accuse them of holding back part of the price of salvation.

"Some persons, when the redemptive process begins, are so wrapped up in material possessions that they do not give up wholly to Spirit; they retain a part of the price. Man must be cleansed thoroughly before he can come into the full light. Once he truly discerns Spirit, material thoughts give way; when the false is destroyed the good is more and more manifest. This is true of every man's spiritual development. If you give yourself wholly to God, He will destroy all the devils that have become part of you. You must give spirit, soul, and body to God. God is everywhere. You can hide nothing from this universal eye" (MD 50).

The Christian community grew rapidly, due in a large measure to the healings wrought by the Apostles. So astonishing were they that news spread throughout Jerusalem, and the sick were carried into the streets in the belief that even the shadow of Peter falling upon them would heal. The excitement spread beyond the Holy City and from neighboring towns the sick and demon-possessed sought the Apostles. "And they were all healed" (Acts 5:16).

Much of the work of the Apostles was done publicly, for they met daily in Solomon's porch, within the very precincts of the Temple. The high priest had warned them against teaching of Jesus Christ. When his warning did not deter them, the Apostles were put in prison:

"But at night an angel of the Lord opened the prison doors and brought them out and said, 'Go and stand in

the temple and speak to the people all the words of this
Life.' And when they heard this, they entered the
temple at daybreak and taught" (Acts 5:19-21).

Later in the day the high priest commanded that
the Apostles be brought before him, and his messen-
ger came back with the startling report that the
prison cells were empty though the keepers were
standing guard. While the Jewish leaders were discussing this strange phenomenon, word was brought
that the Apostles were preaching in the Temple!

Again we are reminded that the human cannot
repress or confine the spiritual. The Bible records
many deliverances similar to this. The underlying
meaning is that when man unifies himself with God,
a spiritual power works for him in ways that are
incomprehensible to human reason and superior to
human might.

Taken before the Sanhedrin again, the Apostles
were commanded for the second time not to preach
of Jesus Christ. Again they refused: "We must obey
God rather than men" (Acts 5:29), Peter declared.
So angry were the authorities that they decided to
put the Apostles to death. Gamaliel, a prominent
Pharisee, opposed this. His counsel was, "Keep away
from these men and let them alone; for if this plan or
this undertaking is of men, it will fail; but if it is of
God, you will not be able to overthrow them. You
might even be found opposing God!" (Acts 5:38,
39).

Gamaliel represents a thought of fairness in the
mind that is willing to give each idea a chance to

prove itself. If an idea belongs to the mortal plane of consciousness, it will be destroyed as the individual progresses spiritually; if it is a spiritual idea, it cannot be destroyed. Were we to attempt to overthrow it, we would be fighting against our true inner Self (God).

Reluctantly the Jewish leaders accepted Gamaliel's advice. The Apostles were released after a severe beating and another threat. But "every day in the temple and at home they did not cease teaching and preaching Jesus as the Christ" (Acts 5:42).

The First Evangelists

Acts 6-8; 9:31-43; 11:1-18, 12

The Apostles were, quite naturally, the ones in charge of the Christian community. It had grown rapidly in the several years of its existence and finally it became apparent that the Apostles themselves could not supervise all the details of communal life. This was brought to light when a protest was made by some of the Greek-speaking members (Hellenists, or Jews of the Dispersion) that partiality was being shown to the native or Palestinian members. The Apostles called a meeting and suggested that seven men (deacons, they came to be called) be elected to take care of all mundane affairs, while they devoted themselves to prayer and preaching. "It is not right that we should give up preaching to serve tables" (Acts 6:2), they rightly said. Of the seven elected, all probably Hellenists and men "full of the Spirit and of wisdom," two—Stephen and Philip—were to play a prominent part in the Christ ministry.

Stephen was the first to attract attention. As he spoke Greek it was his custom to frequent the synagogues in Jerusalem where the Jews of the Dispersion gathered. These synagogues had been built and were maintained by Jews who had returned to the Holy City from localities throughout the Greco-Roman world. Stephen's object was to convince them that Jesus was the Savior.

Stephen was a man of intellectual attainments, an eloquent speaker, and "full of grace and power" (Acts 6:8). Even those who refused to accept what he said "could not withstand the wisdom and the Spirit with which he spoke" (Acts 6:10). They became jealous and angry, even going to the extent of bribing men to report that the evangelist spoke "blasphemous words against Moses and God" (Acts 6:11). Stephen was seized and taken before the Sanhedrin, accused of declaring that Jesus would destroy the Temple and the religious rites established by Moses. Perhaps this was a perversion of Jesus' words, "Destroy this temple, and in three days I will raise it up" (John 2:19).

Stephen defended himself in a masterful speech, tracing the course of Jewish history to prove that God's revelation had never been confined to the Temple, which the Jews considered the center of holiness. "The Most High does not dwell in houses made with hands" (Acts 7:48), he avowed. He accused the members of his race of always being slow to accept the messages and messengers of God, and ended with the accusation: "You stiff-necked people, uncircumcised in heart and ears, you always resist the Holy Spirit. As your fathers did, so do you" (Acts 7:51). They had crucified Jesus, the Righteous One.

The members of the Court, both Sadducees and Pharisees, were infuriated by Stephen's denunciation of them. He was dragged outside the city and stoned. As the missiles rained upon him, Stephen

cried, "Lord Jesus, receive my spirit" (Acts 7:59).
Then, kneeling down, the first Christian martyr
prayed, in words reminiscent of his Master, "Lord,
do not hold this sin against them" (Acts 6:60).

Stephen represents the illumined intellect. He had
a clear mental perception of Truth and had received
a sufficient spiritual quickening to be a dynamic
preacher of the Christ word.

> In that state of mind he is typical of the students
> today who receive the Truth, who perceive it, not with
> full understanding, not with demonstration yet, but
> with an illumination so strong that they become enthu-
> siasts. . . . They do wonderfully effective work in those
> early stages—but their work is done in the enthusiasm
> of the intellect. The full regeneration has not yet been
> established in them (MD 630).

The intellect is argumentative and often brings
about friction both within the individual and from
people. At times we should declare our convictions
boldly; at other times it is wise to be silent. Guided
by the Christ wisdom we shall know when to express
our spiritual ideas and when to keep them to ourself:

> The stoning of Stephen (Acts 7:54-60) also shows
> that the final outcome of exercising arguments and zeal
> continually is to bring about resistance. Stephen is ex-
> tolled as the first Christian martyr, and thousands have
> made themselves martyrs by taking his life as a literal
> example, instead of learning from it that violent mar-
> tyrdom for Truth's sake is the result of zeal without
> wisdom. It is not necessary to be a martyr in the cause
> of Truth. To obviate martyrdom, or useless persecu-
> tion, do not argue, do not dispute, do not let your zeal

run away with your love and consideration for those
who do not see things from the same standpoint that
you do. Even though one sees the error of others, he
should not be too ready to condemn. If it is necessary
to quote Scripture to fortify your cause, do so without
heat; then the hard, material thoughts of those with
whom you are talking will not fly at you like stones
(MD 632).

Present at the stoning of Stephen was an ardent
Pharisee who was bitterly opposed to the Christian
belief that Jesus was the Messiah. His name was Saul.
The death of Stephen served to fan Saul's hatred of
the young sect and he instituted the next persecution of the Christians. So thorough were his methods
of finding and imprisoning Christians that many of
them left Jerusalem to escape him. Saul aimed to
destroy the Christ teaching. Instead his cruelties
served to spread it for wherever the followers of "the
Way" went they told of the Savior.

Philip, one of the seven deacons elected to serve
the Christian community, left Jerusalem at this time.
He is often referred to as the Evangelist to distin-
guish him from Philip the Apostle. He went to
Samaria, the district directly to the north of Judea.

Philip represents power, which is energy, vigor,
might. As power is used by man in his unredeemed
state he works to attain selfish, personal ends. When
we are spiritually quickened, our power faculty becomes the means by which we speak the Christ word,
first to our own consciousness and then to others.
Power also enables us to do His work of healing. We
cannot exercise the dominion and mastery of spiri-

tual man until the power of the human has been
merged into the power of the Christ self.

> And the multitudes with one accord gave heed to
> what was said by Philip, when they heard him and saw
> the signs which he did. For unclean spirits came out of
> many who were possessed, crying with a loud voice;
> and many who were paralyzed or lame were healed. So
> there was much joy in that city (Acts 8:6-8).

News of the many converts made by Philip
reached Jerusalem, and Peter and John went to
Samaria to see this startling development. For centuries there had been enmity between Jews and Samaritans, but now a Jew was preaching to Samaritans
and they were listening to him. The Christ message
was dissolving racial and religious differences. We
know that in the sight of God all men are equal. The
realization and practice of this is the only way to
dissolve human prejudice.

When Peter and John arrived in Samaria they
prayed with the natives who also received the Holy
Spirit. Among the converts was Simon, called the
sorcerer. He was so impressed with the Apostles'
power that he asked to purchase it so that he might
bestow it upon others. Peter's reply was a rebuke:
"Your silver perish with you, because you thought
you could obtain the gift of God with money!"
(Acts 8:20).

This gift is available to everyone and requires no
monetary outlay. Its cost is far greater than anything
of a material nature. God gives freely to those who
give themselves to Him. To turn to Him, to believe,

to understand, and to obey—these insure the release of the spiritual power inherent in the Christ nature of man.

On their return trip to Jerusalem the Apostles stopped at other towns of Samaria and preached the Gospel. Philip was now ready for another assignment from the Lord and it came as a prompting to go to southern Judea. On the road leading from Jerusalem to Gaza, Philip spied a lone chariot. It belonged to a prominent Ethiopian, a man of authority under Candace, queen of Ethiopia. This man was attracted by Judaism. He had gone to Jerusalem to worship, and was returning to his native land. Prompted by Spirit, Philip drew near the chariot and heard the Ethiopian reading a passage from the prophet Isaiah:

> As a sheep led to the slaughter
> or a lamb before its shearer is dumb,
> so he opens not his mouth
>
> (Acts 8:32).

Philip asked if he (the Ethiopian) understood the prophet's words. Seeing that his questioner was a Jew, the eunuch admitted that he did not and asked for an explanation. The Evangelist readily explained that Isaiah was referring to the Messiah who was to come, and forthwith "told him the good news of Jesus" (Acts 8:35). The Ethiopian believed, and stopping the chariot by a stream, he received baptism from Philip.

The journey to a desert region to give a message to

one person brings to mind Jesus' great discourse
given to one, the woman of Samaria. When we are
open to Spirit's guidance, we may be sure that our
word, whether it be heard by many or by one, fills a
definite need and serves a vital purpose.

After leaving the rejoicing convert, Philip went to
Caesarea, preaching along the way. In that large and
important city the Evangelist continued his missionary labors, and we shall meet him again in Caesarea
years later.

The next event related in Acts (Chap. 9:1-31) is
the conversion of Saul of Tarsus, whose life will be
taken up in the next chapter. The date generally
given for this important happening is A.D. 34 or 35,
some five or six years after Pentecost and the beginning of the church. It had grown amazingly in Jerusalem and was made up entirely of Jews, those of
Palestine and also of the Dispersion. Philip's success
among the Samaritans enlarged the Christian fellowship by bringing in many who were part Jew and part
Gentile. Thus a whole new field was opened up, and
Peter was not slow to take advantage of it. He started
on a journey that was to lead to the conversion of a
prominent Gentile, an officer of the Roman army.

Lydda, a town in the valley of Sharon, was Peter's
first important stop. There he met a man named
Aeneas who had been paralyzed for eight years, and
said to him, " 'Aeneas, Jesus Christ heals you; rise
and make your bed.' And immediately he rose"
(Acts 9:34).

Lydda means *strife*. Peter symbolizes faith in the power of Spirit, which has been quickened in us by the example of Jesus Christ. The mission of this faith is to renew the whole consciousness, of which the body is part. Thought is the oversoul of every bodily function. If there is a part of the consciousness that has not been exercised rightly in harmonious thought, the bodily organ of which it is the oversoul will become paralyzed. . . . Aeneas *(praise . . . full of thankfulness . . .)* when no longer bound by cross currents of criticism, faultfinding, and weakness, arises and in the name of Jesus Christ proclaims life, health, and freedom; all strife is turned into constructive, spiritual activity; all desert places in consciousness receive the redeeming power of the living word (MD 28, 29).

At Joppa, a port city not far from Lydda, there lived a woman named Tabitha (or Dorcas). "She was full of good works and acts of charity" (Acts 9:36). Taken suddenly ill, Tabitha died, and her friends, hearing that Peter was in Lydda, sent word for him to come to Joppa. Peter answered the summons and was taken to the room where Tabitha lay. He dismissed the grieving friends, kneeled down and prayed. "Turning to the body he said, 'Tabitha, rise.' And she opened her eyes, and when she saw Peter she sat up. And he gave her his hand and lifted her up. Then calling the saints and widows he presented her alive" (Acts 9:40, 41).

Joppa *(beauty)* is the dwelling place of Tabitha, signifying here an awakened soul-opulence in Christ, or spiritual benevolence. When this spiritual force works too much in the outer consciousness it loses connection with the one life, falls sick, and dies. . . .

The "widows" who stand round weeping typify mixed thoughts, only half established in Truth—half truths; they therefore waste their substance in the without. But when the radiant life of faith penetrates the darkness, all is changed. The grace and the beauty of Spirit are again awakened, and Tabitha (spiritual benevolence) is made alive.

The raising of Tabitha from the dead by Peter teaches us to deny away and put out of mind the belief in failures and lost opportunities (MD 640).

Peter's ministry in Lydda and Joppa resulted in many new converts and he remained in Joppa for a time, living at the home of Simon, a tanner. Caesarea, the capital city of the province under Roman rule, was only a short distance to the north, and Cornelius, a centurion in the Imperial Army, was stationed there. He was a charitable man and a deeply religious one, worshiping the one God. As he was praying one day a vision came to him and he saw "an angel of God coming in . . . to him (Acts 10:3). He commended Cornelius for his righteousness and directed him to send to Joppa for a man called Peter.

The name Cornelius means *unyielding,* and he represents:

That in consciousness which, no longer bound by outer show and formality, truly searches after God. Cornelius typifies that in us which communes with the Father (he was a devout man) and feeds the soul with divine light and love in order to live the spiritual life and to make practical in all ways the understanding of Truth thus gained.

The man who comes and stands before Cornelius is an angel of the Lord, or that high spiritual perceptive faculty within the soul which ever dwells in the presence of the Father; its mission is to bring us messages direct from God, when we have opened our mind to Spirit sufficiently to receive.

In this instance the message reveals to Cornelius (or that in us which is seeking a higher spiritual basis) how to open the way for the light of spiritual faith, here typified by his sending for "Simon, who is surnamed Peter." The *unyielding* attitude of mind is good when it is set upon the attainment of spiritual understanding and practice (MD 157).

Cornelius immediately followed the Lord's direction and while his messengers were en route to Joppa, Peter also had a vision. He had gone to the housetop to pray, and there came to him a vision of a great sheet let down from heaven to earth. "In it were all kinds of animals and reptiles and birds of the air. And there came a voice to him, 'Rise, Peter; kill and eat' " (Acts 10:12, 13). The Jews had very strict rules concerning the eating of animals, and while some of those which Peter saw in the sheet were ceremonially clean and fit for food, others were not. Peter protested, "No, Lord; for I have never eaten anything that is common or unclean" (Acts 10:14). Three times he was told to kill and eat: "What God has cleansed, you must not call common" (Acts 10:15). Then the vision faded. Peter did not know its meaning, but when the messengers of Cornelius arrived he understood that the Lord was telling him to minister to a Gentile.

The gulf between Jew and Gentile then was greater than we can imagine today. To the Jew a

Gentile was "unclean" in his religious beliefs and also in his mode of living. Jews held themselves apart from all association with Gentiles and separatism was strongly ingrained in every pious Jew. Peter's prejudices had to be dissolved, and the vision came to show him that men of another race and religion could also be deserving of Jesus Christ. The Truth is for all who yearn for it and make way for its reception by faith and righteous living.

In the Old Testament, Hebrews or Jews represent spiritual ideas in consciousness. In the New Testament, Jesus, the Apostles, and Jewish Christians typify spiritual ideas. The Jewish leaders and orthodox Jews in general stand for religious thoughts that are bound by materialism and the forms and ceremonies of religion. Being spiritually blind they refused to accept Jesus and oppressed His followers. Gentiles symbolize worldly thoughts. There must be a reconciliation between our spiritual and worldly thoughts, and only Christ can break down the wall of separation. Faith (Peter) has to be convinced that there should be no barriers in the mind that accepts Christ as the living Word. All thoughts (Jew and Gentile) are unified in Spirit.

At the home of Cornelius he, his family, and some close friends awaited Peter's arrival. When he came the Roman centurion "fell down at his feet and worshiped him. But Peter lifted him up, saying, 'Stand up; I too am a man' " (Acts 10:26). One who is established in spiritual consciousness knows that all men are equal and will not permit worship from his fellow man. Cornelius and Peter each told of his vision. Then Cornelius announced that he and the assembled group were ready and eager to hear the apostle.

"Truly I perceive that God shows no partiality, but in every nation any one who fears him and does what is right is acceptable to him" (Acts 10:34, 35), Peter began, and went on to tell of the works of Jesus, the Lord and Savior of all. While he was still speaking the Holy Spirit came upon the entire group. When we yield ourself completely to Christ, new life is immediately imparted to us.

News of the conversion of a Gentile reached the Jerusalem Church and Peter was asked to explain the circumstances leading to this unusual occurrence. He related the whole story and convinced them that God had set His seal upon the conversion of the Gentiles by sending the Holy Spirit upon them. "If then God gave the same gift to them as he gave to us when we believed in the Lord Jesus Christ, who was I that I could withstand God?" (Acts 11:17). Peter's words were irrefutable and the members of the council "were silenced. And they glorified God, saying, 'Then to the Gentiles also God has granted repentance unto life'" (Acts 11:18). Thus Peter drove the first wedge in the solid wall separating Jew and Gentile, and served to make the way at least somewhat easier for Paul to champion the Gentile cause. Problems connected with the terms under which Gentiles would be received into Christian fellowship would come later, but for the time being there was great rejoicing in the furtherance of the Gospel.

The final persecution of Christians in Jerusalem came at the hands of Herod Agrippa, the grandson of Herod the Great, who was now king over most of Palestine as an appointee of Rome. The Jews had always resented the rule of the Herods and Agrippa sought to gain their favor by an attempt to slay all leading Christians. "He killed James the brother of John with the sword" (Acts 12:2). Seeing that this pleased the Jews, Agrippa seized Peter and imprisoned him. It was the time of the Passover and the king planned to execute the chief Apostle as soon as the feast was over. Once before Peter had been in prison and had escaped. Agrippa was taking no chances and set sixteen soldiers, four for each watch, to guard him. "But earnest prayer for him was made to God by the church" (Acts 12:5).

> The very night when Herod was about to bring him out, Peter was sleeping between two soldiers, bound with two chains, and sentries before the door were guarding the prison; and behold, an angel of the Lord appeared, and a light shone in the cell; and he struck Peter on the side and woke him, saying, "Get up quickly." And the chains fell off his hands. And the angel said to him, "Dress yourself and put on your sandals." And he did so. And he said to him, "Wrap your mantle around you and follow me." And he went out and followed him; he did not know that what was done by the angel was real, but thought he was seeing a vision. When they had passed the first and the second guard, they came to the iron gate leading into the city. It opened to them of its own accord, and they went out

> and passed on through one street; and immediately the
> angel left him. And Peter came to himself, and said,
> "Now I am sure that the Lord has sent his angel and
> rescued me from the hand of Herod and from all that
> the Jewish people were expecting" (Acts 12:6-11).

This is one of the most spectacular accounts of the
victory of the Spirit over the mortal. All the force of
world power (represented by Agrippa and the Jews)
was arrayed against the might of spiritual power
(represented by Peter and the praying Christians).
When grounded in faith and sustained by prayer, we
are calm and at peace even in dire straits (Peter was
asleep). Such a state of consciousness is a channel
through which the Lord can move (an angel awakened Peter). We follow divine guidance with implicit
trust (the angel told Peter what to do and he obeyed
every instruction). When we are free of limitation,
we gratefully acknowledge the protecting power of
God (Peter understood that the Lord had sent His
angel to free him). Once again the sacred narrative
reminds us that when we have faith in God, no prison
of any sort, be it sickness, sorrow, or lack, can confine us. The Lord is always present and His deliverance is sure.

Going to the house where his fellow Christians
were praying, Peter knocked at the gate. Rhoda, a
maid, answered, and when she heard his voice she
was so excited that she forgot to let him in! Instead
she ran to the others with the great news that Peter
was there. They were incredulous. How often we
pray and yet are unbelieving of the prompt answer!

Peter continued to knock and when they finally opened the gate there was great rejoicing.

Upon learning that the prisoner had escaped, Herod Agrippa had the guards put to death. The day of his own demise was soon to dawn. While permitting the crowds at a celebration to worship him as a god, Agrippa was suddenly stricken with a loathsome and fatal disease, "because he did not give God the glory" (Acts 12:23). When one elevates the personal above the spiritual and continues to violate the spiritual law by injustice and cruelty, the penalty is great.

> But the word of God grew and multiplied (Acts 12:24).

Chapter 12 of Acts ends our close association with Peter. He figures in the Jerusalem conference (Acts 15), and in Paul's letter to the Galatians he relates Peter's visit to Antioch. There are many traditions concerning Peter. It seems certain that he spent a number of years in Rome and was crucified during the Neronian persecutions, probably about the time that Paul met his death (A.D. 64-65). Papias, one of the early Church Fathers, testifies that John Mark was Peter's companion in Rome and that he wrote the Gospel bearing his name from notes taken from Peter's sermons.

The risen Jesus had commanded His foremost apostle, "Feed my sheep" (John 21:17). Peter never forgot and to the end of his days he gave freely of the living Word that feeds the souls of men. His disappearance from the Gospel story does not mean that faith is no longer needed. It is now to sustain the will as represented by Paul.

A Young Man Named Saul

Acts 9:1-30, 11:19-30, 13:1-3

And the witnesses laid down their garments at the
feet of a young man named Saul (Acts 7:58).

This is our introduction to the one who was to
become the great Apostle to the Gentiles, the man
whose works carried the Christ message to the
Greco-Roman world and whose words have fur-
nished inspiration and enlightenment to Christians
throughout the ages. He was indeed transformed by
the renewing of his own mind. Into that brilliant
mind the dynamic Christ ideal came with such force
that it completely transfigured the narrow and intol-
erant Pharisee into a man whose heart was afire with
love for Jesus Christ.

What gave rise to the consuming hatred that made
Saul consent to the stoning of Stephen who, like
himself, was filled with religious fervor? Saul was
born in the large and cosmopolitan city of Tarsus in
Cilicia in about I A.D. His father was one of the
numerous Jews of the Dispersion and though living
in a predominantly Gentile city, he retained his devotion to Judaism and maintained his home according
to the customs of his race. The Jews who were
brought to Tarsus to promote business were given
Roman citizenship, and though he named his son
Saul, perhaps after the first king of Israel, he also
gave him the Roman name *Paulus*.

The young Saul received his education at home and at the synagogue school where the manual of instruction was the Book of the Law. The training of a Jewish child was essentially religious, and Saul early showed an aptitude for religion. At thirteen every Jewish boy became a son of the Law, that is, responsible for his spiritual welfare, and with his parents' consent, Saul decided to become a rabbi. Before beginning his religious training, however, he learned a trade. This was customary, for the Jews had a maxim that one who did not teach his son a trade taught him robbery. Also, some means of earning a living was necessary for one who aspired to be a religious teacher, as rabbis received no financial compensation. Saul chose to become "a maker of tent material."

When he was about fifteen years of age Saul went to Jerusalem to attend the rabbinical school. There he studied under Gamaliel, the Pharisee, the outstanding teacher of the day. It was Gamaliel who advised the Jewish Council against slaying the followers of Jesus (Acts 5:33-39). Saul became an ardent Pharisee, devoted to the precepts of Judaism and with the determination to dedicate his life to upholding the Mosaic Law as the word of God.

After completing his education, Saul returned to Tarsus as a rabbi. His native city was one of the great educational centers of the Roman Empire, and there as a child and also as a young man Saul came in contact with Greek thought and customs. He must have heard the Stoic philosophers and also have become acquainted with the oriental religions which were so popular in the first century of the Christian era, for his epistles reveal an understanding of them. Saul could not have known it at the time, yet his life in a Gentile city did much to prepare him for the task he was later to assume of interpreting Jesus' teachings to the Greek mind.

Saul was exceedingly conscientious in his endeavor to conform his life to spiritual ideals. He was never tempted by the worldliness of the Sadducees and some of the Pharisees. The young rabbi desired above all else to attain righteousness, and Judaism held that it came from an exact obedience to the Law. This demanded rigid discipline, for the written Law of Moses had been supplemented by hundreds of rules and regulations made by scribes and teachers, called the tradition of the elders. To obey the Law in all its details was practically impossible and resulted either in self-righteousness or despair for the devotee. Superficial teachers were satisfied when they performed the prescribed routine of ablution, fasting, sacrifice, and the like. Jesus came in contact with many such and did not hesitate to denounce them: "Woe to you, scribes and Pharisees, hypocrites! for you tithe mint and dill and cummin, and have neglected the weightier matters of the law, justice and mercy and faith; these you ought to have done, without neglecting the others. You blind guides, straining out a gnat and swallowing a camel!" (Matt. 23:23, 24). Saul was too intelligent a man and too earnest a seeker after God to be satisfied with

outer ritual as a substitute for the spirit of religion.
During the years that he served as a rabbi in Tarsus he
was torn inwardly. He was not at peace with God.
Years later, after he became a Christian, he revealed
the unhappiness of this period of his life (Rom.
7:15-24). The gist of his inner tumult was this:

The Law demanded perfect righteousness, and
this Saul desired to attain. But he recognized human
traits in himself that made it well-nigh impossible to
obey God fully. It was a knowledge of the divine
commandments that had revealed to him his short-
comings: "If it had not been for the law, I should not
have known sin" (Rom. 7:7). He illustrated this
point by saying that the Law specified, "You shall
not covet," yet he found himself often the victim of
covetousness and was unable to control it. It was the
Law that brought his sins to light and thus led him to
self-condemnation. It seemed to Saul that the Law
was actually working to his destruction instead of his
salvation, and he cried:

> For I do not do the good I want, but the evil I do not
> want is what I do. Now if I do what I do not want, it is
> no longer I that do it, but sin which dwells within me.
> So I find it to be a law that when I want to do right,
> evil lies at hand. For I delight in the law of God, in my
> inmost self, but I see in my members another law at war
> with the law of my mind and making me captive to the
> law of sin which dwells in my members. Wretched man
> that I am! Who will deliver me from this body of death?
> (Rom. 7:19-24).

At some time in our spiritual unfoldment we invariably meet just such a conflict. There is too great a gap between our ideals and our power to accomplish, and an inner battle rages between the Spirit and the flesh. (Paul uses the word *flesh* to designate all that belongs to the lower or carnal nature.) The harder we try to force ourself to live by the Spirit, the more resistance the flesh puts up. During this period of his life Saul represents the human will. The will is the executive power of the mind and the use of it is essential, but when the will functions in personal consciousness it becomes willful and attempts to compel conditions it wishes. Saul was trying to take the kingdom of heaven by storm: that is, he was exerting mortal willpower to gain a spiritual blessing. This can never be done, as he was to discover later on.

Inharmony was still storming in Saul when he went to Jerusalem and heard Stephen speak at the synagogue of the Freedmen. Saul had never seen Jesus during the days of His life on earth. It seems likely that while he was attending the rabbinical school in Jerusalem, Jesus was growing to manhood in Nazareth, and during the years of Jesus' ministry Saul was serving as a rabbi in Tarsus. Perhaps he had heard of the sect of the Nazarenes, as Jesus' followers were called by orthodox Jews, but actually hearing Stephen declare Jesus to be the Messiah shocked and infuriated Saul. He considered it his duty to bend every effort to uproot this blasphemy. Backed by the Jewish authorities, he "laid waste the church, and entering house after house, he dragged off men and women and committed them to prison" (Acts 8:3). When many Christians left Jerusalem and spread the Word wherever they went, Saul was even more determined to crush the movement.

News reached Saul that Christians were preaching in Damascus and converting many Jews. He promptly asked for authority from the high priest to go to Damascus and "bring them bound to Jerusalem" (Acts 9:2).

The Acts gives no indication of what was in Saul's mind as he journeyed toward Damascus. It was a trip of five or six days, and Saul had ample time to think of all that had happened. He was not a man to yield his convictions readily, and his whole mind and heart were centered on Judaism as the true religion. Yet he was not thinking of the Law nor of the merciless task on which he was embarked. He was thinking of Stephen. He could not forget the spirit in which this man had met death. Stephen was at peace with his Lord: Saul was not. An intense yearning to know the Truth arose in him. This opened the way for a new revelation:

> Now as he journeyed he approached Damascus, and suddenly a light from heaven flashed about him. And he fell to the ground and heard a voice saying to him, "Saul, Saul, why do you persecute me?" And he said, "Who are you, Lord?" And he said, "I am Jesus, whom you are persecuting: but rise and enter the city, and you will be told what you are to do" (Acts 9:3-6).

Saul saw the risen Lord as He appeared to the
Apostles for forty days after the Resurrection. Regarding this, Charles Fillmore says:

> Jesus exists in a realm of being where the limitations
> of form are dissolved. He lives in the body idea. When
> we have identified ourselves with the Father-Mind as
> Jesus identified Himself with it, we shall see Him face
> to face in His spiritual reality. But while we are in con-
> sciousness of the physical body Jesus appears to us in
> that form. Those who see Jesus in these days as a man
> with form see a mental picture impressed upon their
> souls by Jesus. He "stood by" Paul in the same way.
> Many have seen Him in this mind mirage; but we shall
> not see Him as He is until we awake in His likeness. If
> the mind has grasped the capacity and power of spiri-
> tual ideas, then the appearance of Jesus will be under-
> stood (MD 349, 350).

From that moment Saul was convinced of the
reality and truth of the Jesus Christ presence, a conviction and devotion from which he never swayed.
His conversion is one of the most spectacular in the
annals of religious experience.

Conversion in a religious sense is defined as "a
spiritual and moral change, with conviction, from
what is false or worldly to what is true or godly." It is
the result of devotion to the highest spiritual ideal
one has. Until this time Saul had been completely
loyal to his belief that Jesus was not the Messiah, yet
due to the earnestness with which he did what he
considered right, he earned a greater expanding in
consciousness. This the vision gave him. When we are

faithful to our spiritual ideas, regardless of how limited they may be, the time will come when further light is revealed. For such an intense nature as Saul's, with his background of religious training, illumination came as a blinding flash.

Interpreted, conversion represents a spiritual awakening which unites the human will with the will of God. The Christ, I AM, expresses through "I will." "When man links his will with the principle of divine force he has superior executive capacity. He swiftly brings forth faculties that, under the slow action of human personality, would take ages to develop" (CH 111, 112).

This was the great change that took place in Saul as a result of his vision. Until this time his nature had been that of Saul, who represents the will functioning in personal consciousness. He now takes on the characteristics of the name *Paul,* which means "little, restrained, lessened," and signifies one who is devout, humble, and obedient to Christ. "It should not be inferred that the will is weakened by conversion; it is made stronger in every respect. When the will is acting in harmony with divine law, its work is gentle, and to the superficial onlooker the will seems *little*" (MD 506).

This is the great change that takes place in the consciousness of anyone who surrenders his will to the Lord. In the words of the Psalmist we exclaim:

"I delight to do thy will, O my God;
thy law is within my heart"

(Psalms 40:8).

And as we live daily in conscious oneness with Him, we feel a sense of peace and purpose we had not known before. We walk confidently, secure in the knowledge that His plan is being unfolded in our life.

Paul was blinded by the intense radiance of his vision and had to be led into Damascus. He had intended to enter triumphantly and begin persecuting the Christians immediately. Instead, a shaken man asked to go directly to the room prepared for him in the house of a Jew named Judas "on the street called Straight" (Acts 9:11).

Living in the city was one Ananias, a Christian convert. He was a Jew, and along with other followers of the Way he had heard of Paul's cruelties in Jerusalem and knew that he was coming to Damascus for the express purpose of arresting all Jews who professed Christ. The Lord appeared to Ananias in a vision and commanded him to go to Paul's aid: "For behold, he is praying and he has seen a man named Ananias come in, and lay his hands on him so that he might regain his sight" (Acts 9:11, 12). Ananias hesitated but his reluctance was overcome by the divine assurance that Paul was destined to do a great work for the Lord: "Go, for he is a chosen instrument of mine to carry my name before the Gentiles and kings and the sons of Israel" (Acts 9:15).

> So Ananias departed, and entered the house. And laying his hands on him he said, "Brother Saul, the Lord Jesus who appeared to you on the road by which you came, has sent me that you may regain your sight and be filled with the Holy Spirit." And immediately

something like scales fell from his eyes and he regained his sight. Then he rose and was baptized, and took food and was strengthened (Acts 9:17-19).

This is an outstanding example of complete obedience to spiritual instruction. Charles Fillmore states:

Those who look to the Holy Spirit for guidance find that its instruction is given to all who believe in Christ, and they are drawn together often by the direction of the inner voice, or by a dream, or by a vision. Paul needed help to restore his sight. The brightness, or high potency, of Jesus' glorified presence had confused his intellectual consciousness, and this brought about blindness. He needed the harmonious, peace-giving power of one who understood the inner life, and this power was found in Ananias . . . Ananias was receptive and obedient; doubtless he had received this sort of guidance many times. From the text we readily discern his spiritual harmony (MD 50, 51).

It was truly the Christ wisdom that selected Paul as an apostle. He had all the qualities that make for greatness in Christian ministry—a deep and intense love for God, a zeal for service, tenacity of purpose, loyalty, an education that equipped him to meet men of all races, and unusual ability for organization. He was never for a moment to forget his call to be an apostle of Jesus Christ, and years later he was able to say truthfully, "I was not disobedient to the heavenly vision" (Acts 26:19).

From Ananias, Paul learned of the teachings and works of the Master, and he immediately made public confession of his allegiance to Christ. This was a startling exposé to both orthodox Jews and Jewish Christians. The former were angered by what they considered Paul's betrayal of Judaism and the latter were sceptical of his sincerity.

For a short time Paul preached in Damascus and then withdrew to an area which he refers to as Arabia (Gal. 1:17). He had to think out all that had happened. He had received a commission. Before he could execute it, however, he must understand more fully the One who had given it. Ananias and the disciples in Damascus had explained the basic facts but that was not enough for Paul. He had accepted Christ as expressed through Jesus, and he had to understand the relationship of the Jewish Law to the Christian Gospel. During this time of quietness, probably about two years, he realized that Jesus Christ was not for one nation, the Jews: He was the Savior of all men. Paul never preached as did the Twelve. They were not trained as preachers and were content to repeat the words and acts of Jesus. Paul was to go beyond this and interpret His teaching. Both types of message were necessary and each had its place in spreading the Word.

When Paul's season of retirement was over, he returned to Damascus, preaching Jesus as the Messiah. His increasing success made the orthodox Jews bitterly resentful and they plotted with the political authorities to put him to death. Guards were posted at the gates of Damascus to prevent his departure, but those whom he had converted saved his life by lowering him in a basket from the city walls.

Paul went directly to Jerusalem. He was eager to meet the Apostles, especially Peter. Here also his past clung to him and his very name incited fear and resentment among the Christians. Paul needed a friend badly and found one in Barnabas, a wealthy Jew from Cyprus who had donated his riches to the Christian cause (see Chap. II). Barnabas personally vouched for Paul and presented him to Peter and James, the only "pillars" of the church who were in Jerusalem at the time. Peter took Paul to his home and entertained him during his stay in Jerusalem.

The James here mentioned was one of the brothers (or half-brothers) of Jesus. Like the rest of Jesus' brethren, James did not believe in Him while He lived but acknowledged Him after the Resurrection. James was won to faith by a special manifestation of the risen Lord: "Then he appeared to James" (I Cor. 15:7). Thereafter he rose to high eminence and became head of the Jerusalem church. James was called "the Just."

Paul's welcome by Peter and James dispelled the suspicion of the Christians, and he moved freely among them. His preaching in the synagogues was so effective that the orthodox Jews plotted to slay him as they had slain Stephen. Once again the Christians saved Paul's life by smuggling him out of the city. He was escorted to Caesarea and from there took ship for Tarsus.

The Bible gives no record of the next decade of Paul's life. Presumably he preached in his native city

and the surrounding territory. This could not have
been a happy period for him. In Tarsus he must have
been an outcast from family and former friends, yet
there seemed to be no other place for him to go.
Surely these years called for much patience and
faith. Sometimes we feel that we are ready to do a
work and are eager to do so, but no opportunity
comes. Can we use such trying periods for spiritual
development? Evidently Paul did, for when the door
opened to a larger field he was fully prepared. Again
it was Barnabas who befriended Paul by asking him
to join in the work at Antioch.

During the time of Paul's persecution of Christians in Jerusalem some thirteen years before, many
had fled and some had traveled as far north as
Antioch, in Syria. Antioch was the third largest city
in the Roman Empire and had a mixed population.
There the Christian missionaries had converted
many Gentiles as well as Jews, and when repeated
reports of the growth of the church came to those in
Jerusalem, Barnabas was sent to Antioch to investi-
gate. He discovered that a large segment of the
church was made up of Gentiles and someone was
needed who understood the Greek as well as the
Jewish mind and temperament. Barnabas remem-
bered Paul and went to Tarsus to enlist his aid. Paul
promptly accepted the call to service.

The year was A.D. 45. Paul was about forty-nine
years old and in the very prime of life. His naturally
keen mind had been developed by years of study and
his spiritual experiences had given him understand-

ing and a deep devotion to Jesus Christ. He was
strong and sturdy of body, despite a physical difficulty which he referred to as a "thorn . . . in the
flesh" (II Cor. 12:7). What this was is unknown.
Some authorities think he may have been subject to
attacks of malaria: some believe he had an eye afflic-
tion, but whatever his "thorn" was, it did not inter-
fere with sustained physical activity such as few men
could have maintained. Paul was not attractive in
appearance, according to a description in "The
Apocryphal New Testament." He was "of a low
stature, bald (or shaved) on the head, crooked
thighs, handsome legs, hollow-eyed; had a crooked
nose" (Chap. 1:7). Nevertheless he was "full of
grace; for sometimes he appeared as a man, sometimes he had the countenance of an angel." Perhaps
he is best described by the words of Chrysostom:
"Three cubits in stature, he touched the sky."

That Paul was in all ways more than adequate for
the work to which he had been called was soon to be
proved. Because his will had been completely submerged in the divine will, he was able to speak in the
name of Jesus Christ with such understanding and
courage that he represents the "word of Truth" (MD
507) throughout the years of his ministry.

For a year Barnabas and Paul labored successfully
in Antioch. This is rich in spiritual significance.
Antioch symbolizes "formulated theology" (MD
54). This state of consciousness is hidebound with
old religious concepts and must be released. Until
our ideas of God and our relationship to Him under-

go a great change, it is impossible for us to unify ourself with the spiritual life within our being. The work of unification is to be done by "spiritual imagination and foresight" (Barnabas) and the "word of Truth" (Paul) (MD 98 and 507). It is our ability to image or imagine our relationship to God as that of son to Father that provides the understanding of our innate spiritual potential. As we affirm the word of Truth in faith, the consciousness is freed from its former erroneous beliefs and is made receptive to new and dynamic spiritual ideas.

It was at Antioch that the name *Christian* was first given the followers of Jesus. Bestowed by non-Christian Antiochians as a derisive epithet, it became an honored and beloved name to those who believed in Jesus Christ.

Among the converts was a prophet named Agabus who predicted a widespread famine. Judea was one of the many countries affected. The Antioch church promptly organized a fund for "relief to the brethren" in Jerusalem, and Barnabas and Paul were appointed to deliver it. This they did. When they left Jerusalem, John Mark, a nephew of Barnabas, accompanied them. Though a young man, Mark had long been associated with the Christian cause as the home of his mother, Mary, was a meeting place for Jesus' followers. It was probably in this home that the Holy Spirit came upon them at Pentecost.

A happy surprise was in store for the returning missionaries. Though the church at Jerusalem remained the center of Jewish Christian activities until the fall of the city in A.D. 70, the church at Antioch became the capital of Gentile Christianity. Being predominantly Gentile, its members were free of the restrictions of the Jewish Law. They were more liberal and had a greater vision of the importance of spreading the Gospel. Soon after the return of Barnabas and Paul from Jerusalem, the leaders of the Antioch church gathered for prayer and fasting, and the Holy Spirit said to them: "Set apart for me Barnabas and Saul for the work to which I have called them" (Acts 13:2). Thus the spread of the Word abroad was the result of divine guidance, not human planning. How much better to wait for spiritual direction before undertaking any venture! At the time the little group in Antioch could have no conception of the far-reaching effects of its decision.

The missionaries decided to take John Mark with them as aide and secretary. *John* represents love and the name *Mark* means "shining." "God is love and one of the shining activities of love is its zeal in giving. . . . Zeal and enthusiasm are absolutely necessary to the success of any enduring work" (MD 426). In the beginning of our spiritual labors the qualities represented by John Mark are not always reliable (John Mark deserted Barnabas and Paul at Perga), but if we continue to direct the mind toward Spirit, these qualities become steadfast (John was later reunited with Paul and also served with Peter in Rome).

Christian Pioneers

Acts 13–17:14

Barnabas and Paul selected the island of Cyprus as their first stop. It was the former home of Barnabas and had a large Jewish population to whom the missionaries intended to make their appeal. When they set sail from Seleucia, the seaport of Antioch, their departure was unnoticed by the busy populace. Even they themselves had no conception that their voyage was the initial step in a movement that was destined to change the history of western civilization.

Spiritually interpreted, Paul's missionary journeys represent the activity of the word of Truth in the mind and heart of the individual. When we have been spiritually quickened (i.e., converted) spiritual ideas begin to move in consciousness. Our thoughts turn Godward. As we pray, we feel close to Him and there is a desire to speak His word. Even as the mission of Paul was to spread the Christ teaching throughout the world of his time, so it is the mission of our awakened consciousness to redeem our entire being. "Go into all the world and preach the gospel" is the Christ command. When our soul is afire with the Christ light, we enthusiastically preach His gospel throughout our individual world of mind and body.

This is no easy task and Paul's journeys indicate

the difficulties encountered. The cities and countries he visited and the people he contacted stand for various states of consciousness that need to be taught the Truth. When spiritual ideas permeate the whole mind, much of which is filled with false concepts and negative thoughts, there is likely to be a determined resistance. All of Paul's experiences, the successes and failures, are a revelation of how we react to the higher thought. Paul persisted in his endeavor to bring enlightenment to the Greco-Roman world and we must persist in speaking Truth until our whole consciousness absorbs it. Once the Christ ideal has been accepted, it becomes increasingly powerful. When this ideal is in control, the true church of Christ is established within us.

If we understand that all that happened to Paul is symbolic of what happens in us as Truth penetrates the mind, his journeys become more than historical events. They take on the nature of personal experiences and reveal the necessity of speaking the word faithfully and untiringly. In no other way can spiritual illumination come.

First Missionary Journey
A.D. 47-49 (Acts 13:3–14:28)

Paul and Barnabas landed at Salamis, one of the chief cities of Cyprus. Cyprus represents:

> A fair, frank, honest, just, unbiased state of mind . . . established in a degree of substance; . . . thus it draws to one very favorable and desirable conditions.

> This state of consciousness . . . is not truly spiritual,
> however; it needs to become established in Truth
> in order to bring forth fruit that is abiding . . . Cyprus in
> the individual consciousness is in close touch with intel-
> lectual reasoning (the Greeks) and formulated theology
> (Antioch) (MD 161).

Our consciousness is similar to that represented
by Cyprus when we begin the task of spiritualizing it.
There is no resistance but neither is there any real
interest (Paul preached in the synagogues in Salamis
and received no support). We have to continue our
work (the missionaries crossed the island to the west
coast). At Paphos the Roman proconsul, Sergius
Paulus, invited Paul to speak but a Jewish sorcerer,
Bar-Jesus (whose Greek name was Elymas), made a
determined effort to stop him. Serguis Paulus
symbolizes "the reasoning faculty in man searching
for the things of Spirit (MD 583). Elymas stands for
"the sense thought that tries to counterfeit the
working of Spirit" (MD 197, 198). Here we have
opposing forces in consciousness, a desire to hear the
Truth on one hand and a resistance to it on the other.
The lower state of mind should be promptly called
to account (Paul vigorously denounced Elymas and
decreed a temporary blindness for him). When the
sense thought (Elymas) is rendered helpless we can
listen to the word freely. The intellect is responsive
(Sergius Paulus was converted).

Thus the first convert made by Paul on his
missionary journeys was a Gentile. Throughout his
years of preaching Paul was to learn that Gentiles

were more receptive to his message than Jews. He always went first to the synagogue because he himself was a Jew and he believed Jesus Christ was the Messiah foretold by Hebrew prophecy. Invariably, however, the doors of the synagogue were shut to him. Some Jews believed, but they were a small minority. Even as the masses of the Jews in Palestine rejected Jesus and later persecuted the Christian Jews, so the orthodox Jews throughout the Mediterranean area turned a deaf ear to Paul and did their utmost to hinder his work. It was among the Gentiles that he gathered a following. Many Greeks and Romans heard him gladly, accepting Jesus Christ as their savior and forming the nucleus of the Christian church.

This is not surprising when considered spiritually. The orthodox Jews of the New Testament stand for religious thoughts clinging to the letter of the law and bound to form and ceremonies. A mind filled with such thoughts is the relentless foe of new concepts of Truth. Jesus recognized and deplored this, calling the Pharisees "blind guides" (Matt. 15:14). He declared that the "tax collectors and the harlots go into the kingdom of God before you" (Matt. 21:31). Gentiles represent the human, worldly thought. This is an unredeemed state of consciousness and often sinful, but it is free of dogmatic religious beliefs and frequently willing to listen to Truth. A person may be worldly simply because he is ignorant of spiritual things. He is rarely antagonistic in the same sense as one who knows and deliberately rejects them. Many Gentiles who heard Paul brushed aside his words and returned to their accustomed materialistic interests. They stand for the person who is not yet ready for a higher teaching. Many others welcomed his message and responded whole-heartedly. They stand for the one who is eager for Truth and willing to begin spiritual development. However, much work has to be done before even the most receptive person is on a firm spiritual foundation.

From Cyprus Paul and Barnabas sailed to the mainland of Asia Minor, landing at Perga in the province of Pamphylia. There John Mark left them and returned to Jerusalem. His desertion bespeaks the unstabilized state of mind that abandons Truth when the way gives evidence of hardship.

The missionaries arrived in Pisidian Antioch after a journey over the Taurus mountains from sea level to several thousand feet above. Antioch represents the type of religious thoughts that are antagonistic to deeper truths. This interpretation is borne out by what happened to Paul and Barnabas in the city. On the Sabbath they went to the synagogue. After the prayers and reading from the Torah, they were invited to speak to the congregation. Paul was the speaker and here we have his first recorded sermon (Acts 13:16-41). This is undoubtedly a sample of what he preached in each city to introduce his hearers to the Christian message. His sermon began with a brief synopsis of Hebrew history as a basis for presenting Jesus Christ as the promised Messiah.

God, he said, had always provided for His people and had at last given them a Savior whom, in their ignorance and hardness of heart, they crucified. But He rose from the dead and offers forgiveness and salvation to all who accept Him. This is the Christian message in a nutshell. Christ is the Anointed One, "the only Son from the Father" in whom is everlasting life and who finds full expression in Jesus. When we believe in Jesus Christ and follow Him, our transgressions are forgiven and we are saved from sin, sickness, and lack.

After the meeting many of the people who were present asked Paul to speak to them again on the next Sabbath. On that day "almost the whole city" came to hear him. The sight of the multitude aroused the jealousy of the Jews and they repudiated Paul's teaching. Whereupon he turned exclusively to the Gentiles, many of whom "were filled with joy and with the Holy Spirit" (Acts 13:52). Soon Jewish hostility became so intense that the missionaries were forced to leave the city.

Iconium, some eighty miles east of Antioch, was the next stop. Iconium signifies:

> A group of thoughts of an imaging and receptive (tending to negativeness) character, in the emotional nature. . . . In this group of thoughts, Iconium, the true light is beginning to break. While it is of the natural animal affections and emotions *(breast of sheep),* and is open to both good and error, it is coming gradually into its true Christ light and dominion, despite the apparent commotion that still takes place there at times (MD 293).

The people of Iconium listened to Paul so attentively that "a great company believed, both Jews and Greeks" (Acts 14:1), and because of their faith there was a great manifestation of divine power, "signs and wonders" being done by the missionaries. They remained in Iconium, probably for several months, and again the orthodox Jews stirred up trouble. Upon learning of a plot against their lives, Paul and Barnabas left the city. We can speak the word of Truth just so much at a given time before it meets resistance from old states of mind. Yet when the seed for a higher consciousness has been planted, it will bear fruit later (Paul left a group of believers in Iconium).

The missionaries then went to Lystra and there Paul performed his first recorded healing. A man who had been crippled from birth "listened to Paul speaking; and Paul, looking intently at him and seeing that he had faith to be made well, said in a loud voice, 'Stand upright on your feet.' And he sprang up and walked" (Acts 14:9, 10).

The miracle so impressed the populace that they thought the missionaries were gods. Calling Barnabas, Zeus, and Paul, Hermes, they attempted to offer sacrifices to them. Such adulation was immediately repelled by the two. "We also are men, of like nature with you, and bring you good news, that you should turn from these vain things to a living God" (Acts 14:15). No truly spiritual person will permit others to worship him. He remembers the command:

"You shall worship the Lord your God
and him only shall you serve"

(Matt. 4:10).

The frankness of the missionaries so dampened the
ardor of the Lystrians that a committee of Jews
arriving from Antioch and Iconium had no difficulty
in turning them against Paul. He was stoned and
dragged out of the city for dead. The spiritual meaning of this is given by Charles Fillmore:

> When one has received the spirit of peace and praise,
> and starts out in spiritual ministry with one's vision
> fixed on the idea of one Presence and one Power,
> adverse thoughts and conditions begin to disappear
> [the word *Lystra* means *that which dissolves or
> frees*]. . . . However, often in the dissolving process
> you may awaken antagonism, and therefore meet with
> opposition (Antioch). If one relinquishes one's stead-
> fast vision of the one Presence and one Power, and
> becomes observant of opposition or adversity, one's
> growing spiritual consciousness seems to be stoned to
> death. But the spiritual consciousness cannot be
> destroyed. It revives at the first opportunity.
>
> In meeting opposition, both within oneself and in
> the outer world, one should remember that Spirit does
> not arouse combativeness. Opposition comes from the
> personal. By one's keeping one's vision steadfastly in
> harmony with the one Presence and one Power, one can
> cause adversity to disappear in divine order, and the
> freedom of the whole man will result. As one's con-
> sciousness is thus clarified these same principles
> become effective in one's outer ministry (MD 410).

Derbe was the next city on their itinerary. The name *Derbe* means *"harsh; stinging"* and represents ''wounded feelings, self-condemnation . . . acute suffering'' (MD 171); it symbolizes the unhappy state of mind that is likely to follow a trying experience. Until we attain Christ consciousness, which means complete freedom from the personal, there are times when cruel and unjust treatment affects us keenly. If we have the spiritual stamina of Paul we will continue our work just the same. He preached the gospel and ''made many disciples.''

Upon completing the ministry at Derbe the missionaries revisited the cities in which they had spoken, and they appointed elders to be in charge of the Christian groups that had been formed. Retracing their steps to Perga, they went to Attalia and set sail for Syrian Antioch.

> And when they arrived, they gathered the church together and declared all that God had done with them, and how he had opened a door of faith to the Gentiles (Acts 14:27).

The success of this journey, despite its hardships, signifies a firmer establishment of the word of Truth in consciousness.

The Jerusalem Conference

(Acts 15:1-35)

While Paul and Barnabas were in Syrian Antioch,

some Jewish Christians came from Jerusalem and stirred up trouble in the church. They were called legalists or Judaizers because they insisted that Gentiles must become Jews and abide by all the laws of Judaism, circumcision in particular, before they could become Christians. Christianity was still considered a sect within the parent religion. There were many Gentile converts in the Antioch church who had not conformed to Jewish customs and ceremonial practices; nor had the Gentiles who had been accepted into the church by Paul and Barnabas on their missionary journey.

The stand taken by the Jewish Christians from Jerusalem posed quite a problem for the young church and gave rise to heated arguments. It was a matter that had to be settled promptly if Gentiles were to continue to come into the church. Finally the Antiochian leaders appointed Paul and Barnabas to go to Jerusalem and confer with the leaders of the church there. This meeting is known as the Jerusalem Conference, and the result of it was to have far-reaching effects.

Peter sided with Paul and Barnabas and cited the Lord's command to him regarding the Gentile Cornelius. This swung the discussion in Paul's favor and evidently had much to do with the decision rendered by James, head of the Jerusalem church. He ruled that Gentiles could be accepted as members of the Christian church exempt from the legalistic requirements of Judaism. His suggestion that they be asked to follow four rules, mainly concerning food, did not mitigate the effectiveness of his declaration. In other words, he gave Christianity its freedom as an independent religion, accessible to all people.

Interpreted, this decision represents the activity of judgment which James represents. Spiritual judgment reveals that it is the spirit of the law which is essential, not the letter of it. Jesus denounced the Pharisees for their insistence on forms and ritual and their disregard for true spirituality, saying, "you tithe mint and rue and every herb, and neglect justice and the love of God" (Luke 11:42). Every individual should be at liberty to go direct to Christ in his own way and follow the spiritual precepts laid down by Jesus. Such freedom is upheld by divine judgment.

Second Missionary Journey

A.D. 49-51 (Acts 15:36 — 18:22)

Again in Antioch and later in the same year, Paul proposed a second missionary journey. Barnabas agreed and wanted to take John Mark with them again. Paul refused. His refusal should not be attributed to lack of forgiveness but rather to sound judgment. By his desertion ón the first journey John Mark had shown himself to be unreliable, and Paul, filled with zeał to spread the Christ message, wanted a trustworthy companion. The disagreement over John Mark led to the parting of the two friends. Barnabas and Mark set out for Cyprus and Paul selected Silas (contraction of *Silvanus*) as his coworker. Silas was an early Christian leader, known and respected by the Christian brethren in Jerusalem and probably a Roman citizen.

Spiritually, this change has an interesting connotation. It means that the spiritual qualities that Barnabas represents (imagination and insight) have, for the time being, served their purpose in the ministry of Paul (the word of Truth). Barnabas had discerned Paul's unusual capability when the two met in Jerusalem, when Paul was unknown to the leaders of the church. By calling Paul to assist in the work at Antioch and accompanying him on the first missionary journey, Barnabas had given Paul the opportunity to prove his remarkable talents. The imaging faculty of the mind, coupled with spiritual insight, is necessary in order that the Truth may attain prominence in consciousness. When this has been accomplished there is a separation, symbolized by the parting of Paul and Barnabas. Paul is now accompanied by Silas. The name *Silas* means "wooded" and he represents "a rugged state of mind: also understanding" (MD 619). These qualities give greater strength to the word of Truth (Paul).

The apostle was to have a number of helpers during the years of his ministry. Each stands for a spiritual quality that increases the effectiveness of the word of Truth. These various co-workers stand in a somewhat similar relation to Paul as did the Apostles to Jesus. A strong spiritual consciousness arouses a number of inherent faculties which augment and sustain it.

Paul and Silas visited several of the churches that had been established on the first missionary journey and finally arrived at Lystra. There they found someone to take the place of John Mark, a youth whose name was Timotheus, or Timothy. It is probable that both Timothy and his Jewish mother were converted on Paul's previous visit to Lystra. Of all the companions the apostle was to have in subsequent years, he seems to have loved Timothy the most. In the epistles he sometimes refers to him as a son, and indeed that is the way he felt toward Timothy. The young man returned Paul's affection and proved to be a loyal friend and faithful supporter.

> Timothy represents an idea in us that has its inception in a union between our intellectual reasoning [Greek father] and our inner spiritual qualities of faith and love [Jewish mother]. So we understand Timothy to symbolize inspired reason united with faith and zeal (MD 658).

Having completed his tour of the towns previously visited, Paul wanted to penetrate deeper into virgin territory but he was "forbidden by the Holy Spirit to speak the word in Asia" (Acts 16:6). Then he considered Bithynia. This too was rejected by Spirit. When we put ourself in God's hands and ask for His guidance it is sometimes contrary to a plan we thought was best. Like Paul we should heed this inner prompting and wait for further direction. The Holy Spirit has a better way for us.

Traveling somewhat aimlessly for the moment,

the missionaries reached Troas, a port town on the Aegean Sea near the site of the ancient city of Troy. Looking across the Hellespont they could see the shore of Europe, and a vision came to Paul in which a man from Macedonia urged him to "come . . . and help us" (Acts 16:9). He recognized this as the divine guidance he was waiting for and lost no time in setting sail for Macedonia, a Roman province in Paul's time. As to the spiritual meaning of this call Charles Fillmore says:

> Fervor, intensity, and vehemence are required in order to carry the great and beautiful message of Truth over seeming hindrances to the different centers and states of consciousness . . . Macedonia signifies the enthusiasm and the energy of Spirit, which set the whole man aflame. It is necessary that this phase of the consciousness be cultivated, because without it a passivity sets in that makes one content with the battle only half won.

> Man should stir up his fiery power when he finds himself getting into negative states of consciousness. The vision of the man imploring, "Come over into Macedonia, and help us," is the discernment of the need of stirring up this inner fervor, this great consuming desire of the soul for spiritual understanding and power (MD 412).

At this point in the narrative (Acts 16:10), the first of the so-called "we sections" of the book begins, indicating that Luke, thought to be the author, joined Paul's party at Troas. Luke was a Greek physician, probably converted by Paul earlier in his ministry. The name *Luke* means "luminous; enlightening" and he represents:

> That phase of the intelligence that has to do with keeping the body well.... Paul and Luke working together symbolize the converted will and spiritual illumination united in presenting the healing ministry of Jesus Christ to the entire being (MD 408).

One of the most important and far-reaching steps in the spread of Christianity was taken when these four men sailed for Europe. It meant that the Gospel was to spread to the West instead of to the East, its birthplace. East represents the inner or esoteric nature of man; West, the outer or exoteric. The Christ has being within but must come into outer expression. Jesus taught us to pray "Thy kingdom come . . . on earth as it is in heaven." Only part of our work is accomplished when we recognize and acknowledge the Christ life within. This life is to be used to illumine the mind, heal the body, and prosper the affairs. The word of Truth (Paul) is directed to bring forth the fruits of the Spirit, to demonstrate the powers inherent in man. We fall short of the Christ ideal of a more abundant life unless we speak the word to raise the whole man and bring into outer manifestation the qualities of the spiritual realm. "Faith without works is dead" (James 2:20 A.V.). The faith that rises in the inmost recesses of our being is to be put to work to redeem not only the soul but the outer life as well.

The travelers landed at Neapolis and crossed the mountains to Philippi, some ten miles distant. Philippi was a Roman military colony and a chief city in Macedonia. The Jewish population was so small that meetings were held outside the city near a river. Paul and his companions joined them on the Sabbath. He was invited to speak and made his first European convert, a woman named Lydia. She was a Gentile engaged in the business of selling goods colored with the famous purple dye made from shellfish, so popular at the time. Lydia was a "worshiper of God," meaning that she had accepted Judaism, but when she heard Paul she turned to Jesus Christ and she and the members of her household were baptized. By inviting the missionaries to stay in her home she made it the meeting place of Christians. The name *Lydia* means "travail; contention" and she represents "the travail that the soul undergoes in conceiving and giving birth to spiritual ideas. Spiritual understanding is developed in the feminine realm of the soul" (MD 409).

Philippi represents "a thought center of power and vigor in consciousness" (MD 527). When the word of Truth is spoken consistently there is likely to be resistance from this vigorous power center if its main interest is on the material plane. The Christ word strikes at injustice and human greed, and the mortal thought fights back. Paul healed a slave girl of a "spirit of divination" (she was a soothsayer) and the merchants who owned her, seeing that she could no longer contribute to their ill-gotten gains, took

Paul and Silas to the magistrates, accusing them of
being troublemakers and preaching unlawful things.
They were beaten and imprisoned.

> But about midnight Paul and Silas were praying and
> singing hymns to God, and the prisoners were listening
> to them, and suddenly there was a great earthquake, so
> that the foundations of the prison were shaken; and
> immediately all the doors were opened and every one's
> fetters were unfastened (Acts 16:25, 26).

This contains a practical and valuable lesson in
spiritual living. There are times when we find ourself
in grave difficulty (prison), seemingly through no
fault of our own. We may have tried sincerely to
conform to spiritual standards and yet we are
afflicted by disease or lack. The human way is to
complain bitterly, to feel that God has forsaken us
and to indulge in self-pity. How does the true apostle
of Jesus Christ meet such a situation? He does not
struggle against the injustice: he trusts the Lord for
his release. Steadfastness in faith always pays rich
dividends. We may not see *how* the problem is to be
solved, but God has ways we know not of. Our part is
to hold fast to Him (Paul and Silas prayed and sang
hymns), and we shall certainly be freed.

The missionaries made no attempt to escape even
when the prison doors were opened. This so impressed the Roman jailer that he was converted and
took them to his home. He washed their wounds,
and he and his family were baptized. The next day

the magistrates ordered the prisoners to be released; they were greatly frightened when they learned that Paul and Silas were Roman citizens. Paul refused to leave, until the magistrates came in person and implored the two to quit the city.

Traveling southwest along the Roman road for about a hundred miles, Paul, Silas, and Timothy reached Thessalonica. Thessalonica represents "the burning or heated zeal of the soul in its desire for Truth, but at this phase of unfoldment it is without a sufficient thinking balance to give tolerance and wisdom" (MD 653). When we are in this state of consciousness, that is, zealous for Truth, we will listen avidly and gladly accept it (Paul's message was received with enthusiasm and many were converted). But when opposition arises (the orthodox Jews violently rejected Paul and arrested Jason, a convert in whose home Paul was living, accusing Jason of harboring "these men who have turned the world upside down"), the one who is not yet stabilized in spiritual thought is swayed by the majority belief and deserts the spiritual ideas he has accepted (the converts did not defend Paul and his companion). When this happens in our own experience it is the part of wisdom not to attempt to force the mind to accept Truth ideas for the time being (the missionaries left Thessalonica). They moved on to Beroea and again went to the synagogue of the Jews. Beroea symbolizes:

> The zeal of the soul in religious matters, tempered by good judgment, tolerance, and intelligent willingness to

examine all thoughts presented to it, that the real Truth
may be discerned and received into consciousness. By
understanding is any phase of man's consciousness
watered [Beroea means *watered*] so that the Truth
may take root and grow and bring forth fruit (MD 112).

This interpretation is confirmed by Paul's happier
experience in Beroea:

Now these Jews were more noble than those in Thessalonica, for they received the word with all eagerness,
examining the scriptures daily to see if these things
were so. Many of them therefore believed, with not a
few Greek women of high standing as well as men (Acts
17:11, 12).

All too soon, however, a deputation of Jews
arrived from Thessalonica and stirred up animosity.
Paul thought it best to depart but as the disturbance
was not as serious as in other places, he left Silas and
Timothy in Beroea to continue the work. (Evidently
Luke had remained in Philippi.) Paul took ship for
Athens, some two hundred miles to the south.

Spreading the Gospel

Acts 17:15–19, I and II Thessalonians, Galatians, I and II Corinthians

In leaving Macedonia Paul entered a southern province known as Achaia, which is now a part of Greece. As his ship entered Piraeus, the harbor of Athens, a reminder of the "glory that was Greece" met his eyes. Before him rose the Acropolis with its magnificent temple, the Parthenon, housing the huge gold-and-ivory statue of Athena. For centuries Athens had been the intellectual center of the world and though it had passed the height of its greatness, it was still the Mecca for advanced philosophical and religious thought.

Paul went alone into the city, intending to wait there until Silas and Timothy joined him. Apparently he did not plan to preach, but he could not resist talking about Jesus Christ to any who would listen. Finally he was invited to speak on Mars Hill (Areopagus), the gathering place of philosophers.

In contrast to his usual direct manner of presenting Christ as the Savior, Paul began by complimenting the Athenians on their interest in religion and pointed to the altar that had been inscribed "to an unknown god." This god was the God of the universe, Paul said, who is spiritual in nature and "does not live in shrines made by man" (Acts 17:24). God is the Father of all men and they should seek Him "in the hope that they might feel after him and find him. Yet he is not far from each one of us, for 'In him we live and move and have our being' " (Acts 17:27, 28). God, he continued, does not condemn men for idolatry when they are ignorant but now He requires that they repent, for He will judge the world in righteousness by "a man whom he has appointed" and whom He raised from the dead, Jesus Christ.

The idea of resurrection was met with ridicule by the majority of Paul's hearers. Though a few were impressed, the Christ message did not gain a foothold in Athens during Paul's lifetime.

To all appearances this was a defeat for Paul, and the reason lies in a spiritual interpretation of the incident. Athens stands for the "intellectual center in man" (MD 78). The intellect can be the forerunner of spiritual illumination but when it is given wholly to mental interests, as in the case of the Athenians, it presents a closed door to Truth. It is wise to refrain from further attempts to influence such a mind. When Jesus sent the Twelve throughout Galilee He said, "And if any one will not receive you or listen to your words, shake off the dust from your feet as you leave that house or town" (Matt. 10:14). We do not know whether Paul was familiar with this command but he followed it nevertheless. Very soon he shook the dust of Athens from his feet and went to Corinth.

Corinth was a prosperous and important commercial city. Among the gods, the Corinthians worshiped Aphrodite, the goddess of love. In her name such sensual rites were performed that the city had become known for its immorality. Corinth represents the "love center . . . but this center is largely given over to licentiousness" (MD 156). In spiritual development it is essential that the love center be purified. God is love and when love is degraded the whole being is enmeshed in falsity.

The Roman Emperor Claudius had recently banned Jews from Rome and many had fled to Corinth. Among them were Aquila and Priscilla, a couple with whom Paul was to form a lasting friendship. They too were tentmakers. Paul lived and worked with them and they proved to be of great help to him in his ministry. Aquila and Priscilla represent respectively the *positive* and *receptive* "healing forces of nature that are always at work rebuilding the body and repairing the ravages of ignorant man" (MD 57 and 535). As the word of Truth (Paul) penetrates the body consciousness, the healing forces inherent in the body are aroused. Thus Paul, with Aquila and Priscilla, lifts the whole man to a higher state. Regularly on the Sabbath Paul went to the synagogue where he "persuaded Jews and Greeks" (Acts 18:4). While he was thus engaged Silas and Timothy arrived from Macedonia bringing the good news that a small group in Thessalonica was holding to the faith in spite of persecution. However they were questioning Paul's sincerity because he had not returned to them, and they were also confused regarding the Second Coming of Christ. Paul promptly wrote them a letter. When he began dictating, probably to Silas, he had no idea that he was writing what would probably become the first written book of the New Testament.

The Pauline epistles, thirteen in number if the Pastorals (I and II Timothy and Titus) are included as they generally are, form a large and important part of the New Testament. Next to the Four Gospels (which were not written until after Paul's death—with the possible exception of Mark), his epistles are the most helpful and beloved of the twenty-seven books of the New Testament. In Chapters V, VI, and VII (in which the letters are included), no attempt is made to give a spiritual interpretation of his ideas. Here the purpose is to place them in the time order agreed upon by most Bible scholars, tell something of the conditions that motivated him to write them, and give a brief analysis of each. Some of the matters discussed are not now of interest except as showing the conditions that existed in the infancy of the church, but his profound understanding of the Christ teaching and his insistence on handling practical problems in a spiritual way are of great value to Christians of every age.

A summary of the main points of Paul's theology and how they are related to our own study of Truth is given in Chapter VIII.

I Thessalonians

Paul begins his letter by praising the Thessalonians for their faith under hardships and affirms his love for them, explaining why he has not been able to return to Thessalonica. He then takes up the matters that were disturbing them.

His teaching of the resurrection of the body was an entirely new idea to Gentile converts and therefore they were confused about the *parousia,* or Second Coming of Christ. What would be the state of those who had died before hearing the Christ message, and what would happen to those who were alive when He came? Paul's answer was:

> But we would not have you ignorant, brethren, concerning those who are asleep, that you may not grieve as others do who have no hope. For since we believe that Jesus died and rose again, even so, through Jesus, God will bring with him those who have fallen asleep. For this we declare to you by the word of the Lord, that we who are alive, who are left until the coming of the Lord, shall not precede those who have fallen asleep. For the Lord himself will descend from heaven with a cry of command, with the archangel's call, and with the sound of the trumpet of God. And the dead in Christ will rise first; then we who are alive, who are left, shall be caught up together with them in the clouds to meet the Lord in the air; and so we shall always be with the Lord. Therefore comfort one another with these words (I Thess. 4:13-18).

As no one knew when the Lord would come, Paul said it behooved them to conduct themselves as befitted His followers. He stressed the necessity for strict morality and brotherly love. Most of the converts in Thessalonica, as well as other Greek cities he visited, were Gentiles and had not had the strict moral and ethical training that was fundamental in the Jewish religion. Hence, Paul found it necessary to emphasize morality repeatedly. In practically every epistle this forms a large part of his teaching. He concluded his letter to the Thessalonians by saying, "Hold fast what is good, abstain from every form of evil" (I Thess. 5:21, 22).

The apostle was unprepared for the effect that his words regarding the Second Coming would have upon the Thessalonians. Some in the church were discouraged. They interpreted his words as meaning that Jesus Christ would come again in the near future, and they doubted whether they could possibly develop in themselves the spiritual qualities that would make them worthy to receive Him. Others gave up their ordinary pursuits and depended upon the more stable members of the Christian group for their livelihood, placidly awaiting the return of the Lord who would carry them into heaven. The effect in both cases was demoralizing. When Paul heard of this, probably by a letter from the church, he lost no time in writing again.

II Thessalonians

Paul assures them that the Second Coming is not to be expected immediately. His explanation is somewhat obscure, implying that what he calls "restraining" power (evil) must run its course before the great event would take place. To the conscientious and loyal believers, Paul says that they need only stand firm and continue in well-doing. To those who were shirking their responsibilities, he reminds them that he, Silas, and Timothy had worked to earn a living so as not to be a burden on anyone, and they should do likewise. "For even when we were with you, we gave you this command: If anyone will not work, let him not eat" (II Thess. 3:10).

These epistles deal with two subjects that are of vital importance to us. The first has to do with the Second Coming of Christ. Contrary to Paul's conviction at the time he wrote to the Thessalonians, the momentous event did not occur, nor has it occurred since, although many Christians to this day believe it will take place. Paul's belief was to undergo a drastic revision, as revealed in his later writings. From a physical appearance of the risen Jesus, Paul's concept became that of the indwelling Christ. This he terms the "mystery hidden for ages and generations but now made manifest to his saints . . .,. which is Christ in you, the hope of glory" (Col. 1:26, 27). Charles Fillmore says:

> Let us cease expecting Christ to come in bodily form; let us turn our attention to His risen body already with us. In this way we shall cooperate with Him in setting up the kingdom of the heavens on the earth. . . . Only believe in the omnipresent Christ and you will behold Him sitting on the right hand of Power within your own being! (ASP 171)

The second subject which Paul stresses in these letters is two-pronged: morality and brotherly love. These are fundamental to the Jesus Christ teaching and have always formed a large part of Christian living. The metaphysical teaching, however, has not, on the whole, given them the emphasis they deserve and require. We cannot attain the goal of Christ consciousness merely by acknowledging the indwelling Christ or by accepting the truth that God's will for us is good and praying for that good to be made manifest. Jesus said, "You, therefore, must be perfect, as your heavenly Father is perfect" (Matt. 5:48). So long as immoral thoughts and feelings are allowed to remain in consciousness, so long as injustice, intolerance, falsehood, and hatred reside in us, it is impossible to be the "pure in heart" who shall "see God."

Nor can we love Him without loving His image in our fellow man: "If any one says 'I love God,' and hates his brother, he is a liar; for he who does not love his brother whom he has seen, cannot love God whom he has not seen" (I John 4:20).

These, morality and brotherly love, are the areas in which all Christians, then and now, are most likely to fail. And neither our prayers to know God nor our affirmations for outer blessings can be fully answered until immorality and selfishness are dissolved. Only if our eye is single to Him and our life reflects His qualities shall our whole body (of being) be filled with light. Paul was to reiterate this again and again in letters to his far-flung churches, instructing Christians how to overcome those human deficiencies that ever dog the footsteps of the spiritual aspiraant.

Paul continued his ministry in Corinth and "Crispus, the ruler of the synagogue, believed in the Lord, together with all his household" (Acts 18:8). Even this influence, however, was not sufficient to overcome rising Jewish opposition, and the apostle turned to the Gentiles, speaking from the home of one Titius Justus:

> And the Lord said to Paul one night in a vision, "Do not be afraid, but speak and do not be silent; for I am with you, and no man shall attack you to harm you; for I have many people in this city" (Acts 18:9, 10).

Paul needed this confirmation, as we do at times when we encounter opposition to the work we believe the Lord has directed us to do. If we will continue (as Paul did in Corinth for a year and a half), the day will come when we know it is best to change our field of operation. This is the way the guidance came to the apostle: Gallio, the new Roman proconsul in Corinth, was approached by the orthodox Jews with the complaint that Paul was violating the Jewish law. Though Gallio refused to entertain the charge, Paul was certain that his work in Corinth was completed for the time being.

The apostle sailed to Ephesus accompanied by Aquila and Priscilla. There his preaching was so popular that the Ephesians asked him to remain but, according to the account in the Authorized Version, he had planned to attend an annual feast in Jerusalem and promised to return to Ephesus "if God wills." There is reason to believe that he went to

Jerusalem and then to Antioch. Thus ended the
Second Missionary Journey.

While in Antioch Paul received distressing news of
the churches in Galatia. Some Jewish Christians
(Judaizers) were teaching that the regulations of
Judaism were necessary for Gentile Christians. This
was contrary not only to Paul's conviction but also
to the decision of the Jerusalem Conference. He was
so aroused that he wrote promptly to the Galatian
churches. (Scholars disagree as to the time and place
of the writing of this epistle. Some consider it the
first of Paul's letters, others place the time of its
writing after the Second Missionary Journey).

Galatians

The theme of this epistle is the spiritual freedom
of Christians. A group of Judaizers had attacked
Paul's standing as an apostle on the ground that he
was not one of the Twelve selected by Jesus, and
therefore his word lacked authority. Paul defended
his divine right as an apostle by the revelation of
Jesus Christ to him (Gal. 1 and 2). He assured the
Galatians that they could become Christians without
following the Jewish laws (Gal. 3 and 4). A person is
saved by faith in Christ Jesus, not by the works of
the law (Gal. 3:23-29). This idea he was to develop
more fully in his Letter to the Romans.

Paul cautions them against mistaking freedom for
license. Spiritual living is a challenge to love and
serve one another. Hence, quarreling among the
members of the church should cease:

> For the whole law is fulfilled in one word, "You shall love your neighbor as yourself." But if you bite and devour one another, take heed that you are not consumed by one another (Gal. 5:14, 15).

Though Paul recognizes that there is a conflict within every person between his carnal and his spiritual natures, he urges them not to allow themselves to give way to the former, for this gives rise to many immoral practices (Gal. 5:19-21). Instead they should "walk by the Spirit," for then they will receive the fruit thereof, which is "love, joy, peace, patience, kindness, goodness, faithfulness, gentleness, self-control; against such there is no law" (Gal. 5:22-25).

Third Missionary Journey
A.D. 52-56 (Acts 18:23–21:16)

After spending some time in Antioch, Paul, true to his promise, returned to Ephesus. During his absence Apollos had preached in the city. Apollos was an Alexandrian Jew, a man of education and an eloquent speaker, and he was a disciple of John the Baptist. When Aquila and Priscilla heard him, they "expounded to him the way of God more accurately" (Acts 18:26), and Apollos was converted to the Christ way. He was fired with zeal to preach the Christ word and decided to go to Corinth, taking with him letters of recommendation from the Ephesian Christians. Before his conversion Apollos represents an intellectual concept of Truth intent on dispelling error (he taught repentance). "But when the Christ understanding enters the consciousness, love predominates. Then a true purifying and uplifting takes place" (MD 56).

When Paul arrived in Ephesus, Apollos had left, but twelve of his followers were converted by Paul and received the Holy Spirit. This is sometimes referred to as the "Ephesian Pentecost."

Paul was to spend the better part of three years in Ephesus. Ephesus represents:

> The central, building faculty of the consciousness called desire. . . . The desire is the center from which goes forth the impetus that makes the form.

> The cells that build the form are moved upon by ideas; hence the character of the form is determined by the prevailing ideas back of it. Ephesus was given up to idolatry, superstition, and general materialism. So we find in unregenerate man that the Ephesus center is given over to physical and sense ideas and must be raised to the spiritual by the impregnating power of the word (MD 203).

The sense state of consciousness, as represented by Ephesus, is greatly in need of the spiritual teaching, and Paul's success there signifies that when the word of Truth is given forth with vigor and love, the results are outstanding. Though the more hidebound beliefs resist enlightenment (the orthodox Jews turned against Paul), the soul is largely receptive (Paul's work was so well received that he hired the school of Tyrannus and preached daily). The result of consistently speaking the Christ word is healing of mind and body:

> And God did extraordinary miracles by the hands of Paul, so that handkerchiefs or aprons were carried away from his body to the sick, and diseases left them and the evil spirits came out of them (Acts (19:11, 12).

Healing of the whole man is inevitable when we are receptive to the ministry of the word of Truth (Paul). It is the outer evidence of the raised consciousness *sustained* on a higher level. We should never forget that teaching without healing is insufficient. Jesus commanded His disciples to preach *and* heal. The two are inseparable. The proof of effective preaching or teaching is in the healing of the mind that shows forth in outer ways, especially in bodily healing.

Paul's work in Ephesus gained such popularity that many who had believed in and practiced magic arts burned their books on the subject in his presence. "So the word of the Lord grew and prevailed mightily" (Acts 19:20).

Soon thereafter Paul began to plan for his future activities. He wanted to return to Macedonia and Achaia, then go to Jerusalem and on to Rome. He sent Timothy and Erastus to Macedonia and continued his ministry in Ephesus, waiting for his work to be concluded there. Guidance for his departure came quickly and unexpectedly.

The manufacture of silver images of Artemis, the goddess of the Ephesians, was a profitable business

in Ephesus. In turning the people from idol worship
to Jesus Christ, Paul was hurting the merchants
financially. Finally Demetrius, a prominent silver-
smith, stirred up his fellow workers against the missionaries and a mob set out to find Paul, shouting,
"Great is Artemis of the Ephesians!" Though they
could not locate him, two of his companions, Gaius
and Aristarchus, were seized.

Demetrius represents the material thoughts that
form a material body. When one begins to hold spiritual ideas of the body (the Christ word spoken by
Paul), there is a clash of ideas:

> You cannot change established states of thought
> without some commotion. This commotion is called
> chemicalization. It is not uncommon for the metaphy-
> sician to have a "riot" in his stomach after a denial of
> matter and a powerful affirmation of the purity and
> permanency of Spirit. Sometimes this confusion is so
> great with beginners that they think themselves serious-
> ly ill, when the trouble is merely a riot of the little
> workers who are opposing a change of ideas (MD 170).

This is not an uncommon experience with us and
often arouses fear. But when we understand what is
happening it is cause for rejoicing, for it means that
spiritual ideas are sinking deep into our mind and
will, in time, dissipate the material thoughts we had
about the body. Yet chemicalization is not limited
to thoughts about the body. Whenever spiritual ideas
strike sense states of consciousness vigorously, as in a
sudden intuition or revelation, chemicalization is
quite likely to take place. If we will be still and rest in

the Lord at such times, the commotion subsides and order is restored.

The riot started by Demetrius was finally quieted and the town clerk advised the merchants to bring the matter to the attention of the proper authorities. However, the missionary saw in this incident the guidance he had been asking for and quitted the city.

During his ministry in Ephesus, Paul had carried on a correspondence with the Corinthian church. This church was made up of three distinct types of converts: Jews, some educated Greeks, and many from the middle and lower classes. Their dissimilar backgrounds and beliefs provoked many problems and several factions existed within the church. Paul heard of this unhappy situation and is believed to have written four letters to the Corinthians. Of the two now extant, I Corinthians is one letter but II Corinthians contains portions of three letters. The order of their writing is believed to be: *(A)* II Corinthians 6:14–7:1, *(B)* I Corinthians, *(C)* II Corinthians 10-13, and *(D)* II Corinthians 1-9 (exclusive of *A* and written later from Macedonia.)

Letters to Corinth

(A)—II Corinthians 6:14-7:1: This is only a portion of a letter, the remainder of which has been lost. The theme is morality. Paul admonishes the Corinthians to put aside immoral practices. "**Let us cleanse ourselves from every defilement of body and spirit, and make holiness perfect in the fear of God**" (II Cor. 7:1).

In answer to this the church wrote asking a number of questions. Paul's reply was,

(B)—I Corinthians: This is a lengthy letter and in it Paul discusses a variety of subjects. The first and most pressing was the unification of four factions that had arisen in the church, that is, those who followed Paul, Cephas (Peter), Apollos, and others who took the name of Christ. He reminds them that the Gospel is the good tidings of salvation through Christ to all. Christian teachers are divinely appointed and should work in harmony. One teacher should not be selected to the exclusion of others:

> What then is Apollos? What is Paul? Servants through whom you believed, as the Lord assigned to each. I planted, Apollos watered, but God gave the growth (I Cor. 3:5, 6).

How important it is for us to remember this! Each one has his own work to do in life, and in God's sight it is of equal importance to that done by any person. The Lord will always give the increase if we are faithful to our given task.

The next two chapters deal with the necessity of moral conduct (I Cor. 5 and 6). Then Paul goes into the subject of marriage and divorce (I Cor. 7). He is anything but a strong advocate of marriage, observing, "But if you marry, you do not sin . . . Yet those who marry will have worldly troubles, and I would spare you that" (I Cor. 7:28). However, if people marry they should remain together throughout life (I Cor. 7:10).

In the next three chapters (I Cor. 8–10), Paul discusses in particular the eating of animals sacrificed to idols, but uses this as a springboard to emphasize the point that the Christian should not do anything that sets a bad example to others (I Cor. 8:13). Nor should the Christian ever feel that he is tempted beyond his strength (I Cor. 10:13). If in whatever one does, he does it "to the glory of God" (I Cor. 10:31), he will give no occasion for stumbling to anyone.

In Chapter 11 Paul takes up proper dress and conduct of men and women in the church, also the partaking of the Lord's Supper. At this time the Supper was a full meal, and many came to eat instead of worship. This was not to be done (I Cor. 11:27).

The next subject is spiritual gifts (I Cor. 12:1-11). One gift is no greater than another, for all come from the same Spirit. Yet there is a still greater gift, and in one of the most beautiful and profound chapters in the Bible, Paul extols love (I Cor. 13). Henry Drummond, who gives such a fine interpretation of it, is reputed to have said that if one would read this chapter every day for a month, it would change his entire life.

In Chapter 14 Paul explains the desirability of prophecies, by which he means preaching and teaching, over "speaking in tongues," though the latter is not to be forbidden. "But all things should be done decently and in order" (I Cor. 14:40).

Chapter 15 takes up the subject of resurrection.

This must be accepted for it is fundamental to belief in Christ:

> Now if Christ is preached as raised from the dead, how can some of you say that there is no resurrection of the dead? But if there is no resurrection of the dead, then Christ has not been raised; if Christ has not been raised, then our preaching is in vain and your faith is in vain. . . . Then those also who have fallen asleep in Christ have perished. If for this life only we have hoped in Christ, we are of all men most to be pitied.

> But in fact Christ has been raised from the dead, the first fruits of those who have fallen asleep (I Cor. 15:12-20).

Then Paul continues to speak of the resurrection of the body of believers, which is so often quoted in funeral services (I Cor. 15:40-49).

The epistle concludes with a plea for contributions for the church in Jerusalem (I Cor. 16).

Paul sent this letter to Corinth by Timothy but it seems he was unable to handle the rival factions, and Paul himself paid a hurried visit to the Corinthian church. It was an unhappy time for he was insulted and ridiculed by one of the members. Upon his return to Ephesus, Paul wrote a third letter to Corinth:

(C)—II Corinthians 10—13: Paul sternly defends his authority as an apostle ordained by Jesus Christ, but he pleads for their understanding of his love for them. He tells of his great spiritual experience, how he "was caught up into Paradise . . . and he heard things that cannot be told, which man may not

utter" (II Cor. 12:3, 4). He says he might have boasted of this were it not for the physical ailment which he calls a "thorn . . . in the flesh" and which ever reminds him of his need of humility. He prayed three times that it be removed but the Lord said to him: "My grace is sufficient for you, for my power is made perfect in weakness" (II Cor. 12:9). Paul continued:

> I will all the more gladly boast of my weaknesses, that the power of Christ may rest upon me. For the sake of Christ, then, I am content with weaknesses, insults, hardships, persecution, and calamities; for when I am weak, then I am strong (II Cor. 12:9, 10).

Believing as we do in Truth that God's will for man is health, we may wonder why Paul was not healed. He received the illumination that God's grace is sufficient, but are not the elements of love, peace, power, health, supply, and so on inherent in His grace? Paul evidently has a limited concept of grace as applying to the body. Perhaps to him grace meant God's support in his ministry. He was confident that the Lord had sent him to preach the Gospel but he apparently believed that this was all he should expect. His reaction of glorying in weaknesses and welcoming persecutions and distress shows that the ideas of sacrifice and martyrdom were still strong in his consciousness.

It is undeniably true that often in times of human weakness we are spiritually strong. We are prone to pray more when in difficulties, for we have greater need for our Lord. Our very dependence upon Him and our awareness of His presence gives us greater strength than the human can afford.

In a sense Paul was healed, not of his physical ailment but of his worry concerning it. The thorn in his flesh seems to have had no detrimental effect upon his general health, and his arduous physical exertions were such as few men could endure. You and I have seen those who, despite a physical handicap, have accomplished more by their love for God and faith in Him than does the average person with a strong body. Their human weakness has been secondary to their spiritual stamina. No one of us has yet attained the perfection to which we aspire, but to be able to do His work in spite of infirmities is the mark of a Christ-centered individual.

After Paul left Ephesus he went to Macedonia. At Philippi he met Titus, who had delivered the third letter to the Corinthians. Titus relayed the good news that the offending member of the church had been punished and that order was restored. He also told Paul that the Corinthians held him in high esteem and were eager to hear from him. Whereupon the apostle wrote his final letter to Corinth:

(D)–II Cor. 1-9): This is a letter of affection and reconciliation. It shows Paul's deep love for the church and his concern, likewise his spirit of forgiveness for the member who had heaped insults upon him:

> For such a one this punishment by the majority is
> enough; so you should rather turn to forgive and com-
> fort him, or he may be overwhelmed by excessive sor-
> row. So I beg you to reaffirm your love for him (II Cor.
> 2:6-8).

One of the surest signs of a Christlike character is
the willingness and ability to forgive those who have
hurt us. The human self bitterly resents injustice and
defends its antagonism toward the offender. There is
the deep-seated desire to pay back in the same coin.
But the necessity for forgiveness plays a large part in
Jesus' teaching as well as Paul's. Jesus makes it a
prerequisite for prayer: "Whenever you stand praying, forgive, if you have anything against any one"
(Mark 11:25). He does not qualify His statement by
excusing those who think they have grounds for
resentment. We are to forgive regardless of the wrong
done to us.

Jesus also makes the Father's forgiveness of us
dependent upon our forgiveness of others: "Forgive
us our debts as we also have forgiven our debtors"
(Matt. 6:12). We all have done many things for
which we need God's forgiveness. The law is that as
we give, so shall we receive. To be able to give love,
which is what we want to receive, we need only to
ask His help. It is always forthcoming. By His grace
we are raised above human resentment and our consciousness is cleansed and purified. We are free of the
tension and strain that an unforgiving spirit inflicts
upon the mind and heart. If the offender is remorse-
ful, let our forgiveness be speedy; even if he is not, let

us forgive him anyway. "Do not let the sun go down on your anger" (Eph. 4:26), either for God's sake or for your own well-being.

In his letter Paul goes on to urge the Corinthians to receive God's grace in thankfulness of heart, remembering that the day of salvation is near at hand. They are to give no offense in anything, lest reflection be cast on the church. They should conduct themselves in all ways as "servants of God" (II Cor. 6:4).

This part of II Corinthians closes with a plea for contributions for the Jerusalem Church:

> He who sows sparingly will also reap sparingly, and he who sows bountifully will also reap bountifully. Each one must do as he has made up his mind, not reluctantly or under compulsion, for God loves a cheerful giver (II Cor. 9:6, 7).

Days of Trial

Letter to the Romans
Acts 20–26

Shortly after the final letter to Corinth was sent, Paul paid this church another visit. While there he wrote the Letter to the Romans. This differs from Paul's letters to churches he had founded and whose members he knew personally. He had never been to Rome and his letter is couched in more formal language.

The founder of the Roman Church is unknown. That it was none of the Twelve Apostles seems certain, but a clue is given in Acts: there were "visitors from Rome" (Acts 2:10) in Jerusalem on the day of Pentecost when the Holy Spirit came upon the followers of Jesus. Perhaps one of these, hearing Peter speak, carried the Gospel message back to the capital of the Roman Empire.

Even at this early date the church in Rome was important. Though composed of both Jews and Gentiles, the latter were in the majority. Paul wanted to give these Christian converts the true meaning of the Savior's teaching, to protect them from those who insisted that compliance with the Jewish law was necessary for Christians.

In reading Paul's letters, and especially that to the Romans, we may jump to the conclusion that the lengthy discussion concerning Jew and Gentile has little meaning for us today. But considered spiritually, we see that Paul is really contrasting two types of religious people. One type thinks he is satisfying his spiritual obligation by acknowledging God and fulfilling certain outer obligations; the other realizes that his professed faith demands a complete change within himself, the proof of which is shown in outer ways also. Through the prophet Isaiah the Lord speaks of those who "draw near with their mouth and honor me with their lips," but whose "hearts are far from me" (Isa. 29:13). When we read Paul's letter in the light of its being a plea to love God to the extent of giving ourself to Him, we understand that he is dealing with a subject that is of the utmost importance to every spiritual aspirant.

Romans

The theme of this epistle is "justification by faith." The word *justification* means, literally, "vindication," or in other words, absolution; that is, one charged with a crime who establishes his innocence is thereby justified. As Paul uses the word it means God's pardon for our sins and His acceptance of us because of the righteousness we receive from Christ by our faith in Him.

Paul contends that all have fallen short of righteousness (Rom. 1–2): Gentiles because of their worship of idols and immoral living, and Jews by their insistence on the works of the Law and their disregard for the true spirit of it.

Justification, Paul says, can come only by faith in Jesus Christ (Rom. 3–5). Abraham received God's promise by faith before the Law was given. Therefore, the Jews are in error in considering the legalistic requirements of the Law as essential. Adam (mortal man) disobeyed God and by him sin and death befell mankind. By the second Adam (Jesus, the Christ) came righteousness and life:

> If, because of one man's trespass, death reigned through that one man, much more will those who receive the abundance of grace and the free gift of righteousness reign in life through the one man Jesus Christ (Rom. 5:17).

Sin is incompatible with the new life in Christ (Rom. 6–8). The Law served a helpful purpose for it revealed to man his own iniquities: "If it had not been for the law, I should not have known sin" (Rom.7:7). Paul's own struggle with the rigid provisions of the Law is graphically described in the last half of Chapter 7. The believer must be joined with Christ to attain righteousness.

> For the law of the Spirit of life in Christ Jesus has set me free from the law of sin and death. For God has done what the law, weakened by the flesh, could not do: sending his own Son in the likeness of sinful flesh and for sin, he condemned sin in the flesh, in order that the just requirement of the law might be fulfilled in us, who walk not according to the flesh but according to the Spirit (Rom. 8:2-4).

Both Jew and Gentile are worthy of salvation (Rom. 9—11). By the Jews' failure to accept Christ they hindered themselves. Claiming to be of the seed of Abraham is insufficient. Many Israelites were rejected, God choosing only a remnant for salvation. But by the Jews' rejection of Christ a divine purpose was served, for then the Gospel was given to Gentiles. Gentiles should not feel superior to Jews, however, for God's salvation is extended to both.

Not all who accept Christ receive salvation. Their faith must be exemplified in their life and conduct (Rom. 12—15:13). A full and strong presentation of Paul's deeply spiritual and lofty ethical teaching is given in these chapters, one of the most beautiful of which is:

> Repay no one evil for evil, but take thought for what is noble in the sight of all. If possible, so far as it depends upon you, live peaceably with all. Beloved, never avenge yourselves, but leave it to the wrath of God; for it is written, "Vengeance is mine, I will repay, says the Lord." No, "if your enemy is hungry, feed him; if he is thirsty, give him drink; for by so doing you will heap burning coals upon his head." Do not be overcome by evil, but overcome evil with good (Rom. 12:17-21).

Paul has much to say about the Christian's duty toward God, the church, and society, and he concludes with the benediction, "May the God of hope fill you with all joy and peace in believing, so that by the power of the Holy Spirit you may abound in hope" (Rom. 15:13).

In the remainder of the letter Paul tells of his

activities, his plans for the future, and sends greetings to and from various persons (Rom. 16).

The apostle was eager to take the contributions he had gathered from several Gentile churches to the Jerusalem brethren. He first planned to leave Corinth by ship and go direct to Syria but a plot hatched against him by the Jews made it advisable for him to go through Macedonia into Asia. Luke evidently joined him in Philippi, for again the narrative in Acts uses the familiar "we." The two sailed to Troas where they were met by a group of loyal followers: Sopater of Beroea, Aristarchus and Secundus of Thessalonica, Gaius of Derbe, Timothy, Tychicus, and Trophimus from Asia. These had been converted by Paul and had assisted him at various times in his ministry. Like David and Jesus, Paul was able to inspire great devotion from others. Metaphysically, each of these men represents a quality in consciousness that has been lifted up by the word of Truth (Paul).

At Troas the Christians assembled and Paul preached to them until midnight. One of them, a young man named Eutychus who was sitting in the window, dropped off to sleep and fell three flights to the ground. He was taken up for dead "but Paul went down and bent over him, and embracing him said, 'Do not be alarmed, for his life is in him' " (Acts 20:10).

The name *Eutychus* means "fortunate" and he signifies:

The understanding that the youthful energies of the organism can be quickened into new life again even after they appear to be utterly dead . . . Man is indeed *fortunate* in having the word of Truth (indicated here by Paul) always at hand, since by the word of Truth he can speak his whole being into newness and fullness of life (MD 210).

The apostle wished to be in Jerusalem for the Feast of Pentecost and as the time was now short, he asked the elders of the Ephesus church to meet him in Miletus. After speaking of his several years of service with them he said:

And now, behold, I am going to Jerusalem, bound in the Spirit, not knowing what shall befall me there; except that the Holy Spirit testifies to me in every city that imprisonment and afflictions await me. But I do not account my life of any value nor as precious to myself, if only I may accomplish my course and the ministry which I received from the Lord Jesus, to testify to the gospel of the grace of God (Acts 20:22-24).

Paul warned them against false teachers and commissioned the elders to "feed the church of the Lord" (Acts 20:28), pointing out his own service to them:

In all things I have shown you that by so toiling one must help the weak, remembering the words of the Lord Jesus, how he said, "It is more blessed to give than to receive" (Acts 20:35).

The test of a true Christian is in the example he sets. As Jesus said, "If you know these things, blessed are you if you do them" (John 13:17). When the word of Truth (Paul) is allowed to infiltrate our mind and heart, we want to be of service to those in need and find great joy in being able to give.

From Miletus Paul and Luke sailed to Tyre where they spent seven days with certain disciples, and then pressed on to Caesarea. There they were the guests of Philip, the Evangelist.

It is recorded:

> A prophet named Agabus came down from Judea. And coming to us he took Paul's girdle and bound his own feet and hands, and said, "Thus says the Holy Spirit, 'So shall the Jews at Jerusalem bind the man who owns this girdle and deliver him into the hands of the Gentiles.' " When we heard this, we and the people there begged him not to go up to Jerusalem. Then Paul answered, "What are you doing, weeping and breaking my heart? For I am ready not only to be imprisoned but even to die at Jerusalem for the name of the Lord Jesus" (Acts 21:10-13).

We might wonder why Paul disregarded this warning. It seems clear he felt the good he hoped to accomplish would more than justify his action. He believed that the donations he was taking to the church in Jerusalem from Gentile churches would serve to bring about a spirit of oneness between Jewish and Gentile Christians and prove that in Christ all are one. To achieve this end Paul was willing to face whatever difficulty might arise. Jesus had known that He would be killed if He went to Jerusalem for the Passover but that did not prevent His going. It is not unusual for the indwelling Spirit to warn us that a test is in store. Can we face it calmly and with faith? Paul's personal safety was not important to him; the work he had been commissioned to do by his Lord was important. There is no courage greater than that born of the conviction that we are doing God's will.

Charles Fillmore gives the following interpretation:

> Paul's going to Jerusalem represents the word of Truth as going into the spiritual consciousness, proclaiming the I AM doctrine of Jesus Christ, just as Paul in all his missionary trips represents the word of Truth going into the various parts of the consciousness proclaiming this I AM doctrine of the Christ. The spiritual center (Jerusalem) is under the dominance of the Jews who cling to the Mosaic law and make a great religious outcry against the new kingdom that the I AM or Christ proposes to set up. We are not to let the old religious convictions and teachings deter us from proclaiming that which we know to be true. Jesus Christ is King of the Jews (our religious ideas), and Paul, with his true words, must go without fear of results into the most holy parts and there plant the seeds of the new church, or new state of consciousness (MD 507-508).

Upon his arrival in Jerusalem, Paul was gladly received by the church. The leaders, however, told him that many Jewish Christians believed he advocated that the Jews coming into Christianity should discontinue their Jewish religious practices. This was untrue but in order to clarify his position and convince them he was still a Jew, Paul associated himself with four men taking the Nazarite vow for purification and its observance of exacting ritual.

While Paul was in the Temple some orthodox Jews from Asia Minor saw him and were infuriated. They knew he had preached that the Law was not necessary for Gentile converts. Paul was also charged with defiling the Temple by bringing a Gentile into the inner courts. This was not so. The real reason for their animosity was that the orthodox Jews despised Paul and were willing to resort to any means to destroy him. He was seized and beaten by a frenzied mob. Roman soldiers stationed at the fortress-castle of Antonio, adjoining the Temple, saw the riot and took Paul into custody. At his request he was allowed to speak to the crowd. He reminded them that he was a Jew and at one time had been so zealous for the Law that he persecuted the Christians. Again he related the story of his conversion and said that he had tried to convert Jews but that when they rejected him in city after city, he had turned to the Gentiles. With this the mob cried, "Away with such a fellow from the earth! For he ought not to live" (Acts 22:22).

Interpreted, this means that when one is obsessed by dogmatic religious beliefs (represented by the orthodox Jews), he hates the word of Truth (Paul). His consciousness is closed to any new ideas and he insists on adhering strictly to the letter of the law. This is insufficient: "the written code kills, but the

Spirit gives life" (II Cor. 3:6). As the word of Truth
is presented to such a person it arouses violent opposition and an intense desire to destroy the new idea
which runs counter to his cherished beliefs and tra-
ditional customs.

By letting Paul speak to his accusers, the Roman
officer hoped to find out the charge against him, but
he was unable to make any sense of the matter. He
decided to have the apostle examined by torture.
Paul was bound and about to be scourged when he
revealed that he was a Roman citizen and could not
lawfully be bound. This declaration led to his
prompt release from thongs and he was treated
courteously. But the question of what crime the
Jews were charging him with still remained a puzzle
to the Roman, and he consented to Paul's trial before the Sanhedrin, the Jewish court.

Here Paul's appearance brought about a sharp disagreement between Sadducees and Pharisees. The
subject of the Resurrection was a bone of contention
between them, and when Paul injected it in pleading
his case, the Sadducees denounced him and the Pharisees upheld him. The ensuing argument threw the
court into such a turmoil that Paul's life was endan-
gered. Again the Roman officer intervened and put
the apostle in prison. That night Paul was comforted
by a vision of the Lord who stood by him and said,
"Take courage, for as you have testified about me at
Jerusalem, so you must bear witness also at Rome"
(Acts 23:11).

Interpreted, this conveys the thought that, during

those periods when speaking the Truth arouses opposition and even persecution from those who hold to beliefs in sharp disagreement with ours, we should remember that this is a part of our spiritual ongoing. Jesus was aware that it would happen and said:

> "Blessed are you when men revile you and persecute you and utter all kinds of evil against you falsely on my account. Rejoice and be glad, for your reward is great in heaven" (Matt. 5:11, 12).

By being faithful to the Truth that the indwelling Christ has revealed to us, we gain our reward "in heaven" or through the revelation that He is truly with us and is our protection.

Sometimes the persecution is an inward struggle between our spiritual ideals and those personal states of mind that are still clinging to old beliefs. At such times it seems we are unable to find at-one-ment with our Lord and our God.

> "In returning and rest you shall be saved;
> in quietness and in trust shall be your strength"
> *(Isa. 30:15)*.

It was in the stillness of the night that the Lord came to Paul. It is when we are in a passive and receptive state of consciousness that we feel His presence. "Be of good cheer."

While Paul was under the protection of the Roman guard, a plot was hatched by more than forty orthodox Jews to kill him at the first opportunity.

They asked the Roman officer to let Paul appear again before the Sanhedrin, planning to ambush him as he was led to the court. But, by some means, Paul's nephew discovered the plot and told Paul. Whereupon the officer promptly sent Paul to the Roman governor, Felix, in Caesarea, under guard.

Again Paul's life was saved in a miraculous way. Surely it was the power of Christ moving in this situation that caused one person (Paul's nephew) to upset the plans of many (the forty or more who had vowed to slay the apostle). Whenever it appears that we have so little and our enemy so much, we should remember how Gideon with his three hundred soldiers routed the army of the Midianites, and that God's promise to His own is, "five of you shall chase a hundred, and a hundred of you shall chase ten thousand" (Lev. 26:8).

A few days later Ananias, the high priest, with several members of the Sanhedrin came to Caesarea and appeared before Felix. They charged Paul with being "an agitator among all the Jews throughout the world, and a ringleader of the sect of the Nazarenes," saying, "He even tried to profane the temple" (Acts 24:5, 6). The apostle defended himself against the three charges of sedition, heresy, and sacrilege. As to the first, he stated that he had been in Jerusalem less than a week and had not gathered a crowd nor addressed an assembly. As to heresy, he frankly confessed that he was a Christian but as such he still accepted the beliefs of the Jews and revered their scriptures:

"Having a hope in God which these themselves accept, that there will be a resurrection of both the just and the unjust. So I always take pains to have a clear conscience toward God and toward men" (Acts 24:15, 16).

As to the charge of sacrilege, Paul said that he had been in the Temple performing sacred rites when he was falsely accused and arrested. Moreover, his accusers were not present, and the high priest and those with him were incompetent witnesses. The Sanhedrin had already investigated his case and found that his only fault was his belief in the doctrine of the Resurrection, which many of the members of the court also believed.

Paul's defense was unanswerable but, wishing to please the Jews, Felix said he would withhold his decision until the arrival of the Roman officer who had sent the apostle to Caesarea. Also Felix was in hopes that Paul's friends would offer a gift of money for his release:

> Then he gave orders to the centurion that he [Paul] should be kept in custody but should have some liberty, and that none of his friends should be prevented from attending to his needs (Acts 24:23).

Within a short time Paul was again called before Felix and his wife, Drusilla, who was a Jewess. At that time Paul was questioned concerning his beliefs:

> And as he argued about justice and self-control and future judgment, Felix was alarmed and said, "Go away

for the present; when I have an opportunity I will
summon you" (Acts 24:25).

Felix was a man of ignoble character, corrupt in
politics and immoral in his personal life. He represents the "twin faculties, will and understanding,
functioning in sense consciousness. The word Truth
(Paul) did not move the will but disturbed the understanding which was 'terrified' " (MD 216).

Paul remained in prison for two years. Caesarea
symbolizes the intellect and Paul's imprisonment
there "indicates that the dominating force of the will
[Caesar represents the personal will] had confined
the expression of Truth to the intellectual . . . realm
in consciousness" (MD 508).

It seems inconsistent that the mighty word of
Truth should be confined by the human intellect,
yet this enigma can and does occur in the experience
of all who walk the spiritual path. The divine side of
our nature is greater than the human side, but often
the latter dominates. Paul's imprisonment in Caesarea is a case in point. He was a far greater man than
Felix, yet Felix held the upper hand. Humanly
speaking, Paul must have chafed under this confinement when he longed to be spreading the Gospel.
But though he was helpless outwardly, he made
these years a time of inward spiritual activity which
further subordinated intellect to Spirit. His height-
ened spiritual realization is reflected in his later
epistles.

We invariably encounter a similar experience

somewhere on the path. Then we have a chance to develop one of the greatest of divine virtues, patience. We would like to be about our Father's business, thinking that this means doing good works, but often His business is accomplished when we are quiet and patiently labor with our own consciousness. Periods of rest are equally as necessary as periods of outer service. We need to learn to go within to receive of God as well as to go without to help others. Jesus said: "I came from the Father and have come into the world; again, I am leaving the world and going to the Father" (John 16:28). This swinging in to God and then swinging out into the world is the perfect rhythm of the soul. When times of enforced idleness come, we should understand that they provide the opportunity to solidify the realizations we have had in days of doing His work in the world.

At the end of the two years Porcius Festus succeeded Felix as Roman governor. Festus was a man of higher character than Felix and a better administrator. Shortly after his appointment Festus went to Jerusalem. The orthodox Jews called his attention to the Jewish prisoner Paul, who, they said, was a criminal and should be sent to Jerusalem for trial before their court; they were "planning an ambush to kill him on the way" (Acts 25:3). Festus insisted that they come to Caesarea and prefer charges. They complied but the Book of Acts gives no details of this trial, merely stating that they brought "against him many serious charges which they could not prove" (Acts 25:7). However, Festus wished to please the Jews and asked Paul if he would consent to go to Jerusalem for trial. Knowing that he would be slain, Paul took advantage of his right as a Roman citizen and said, "I appeal to Caesar" (Acts 25:11).

Festus could not refuse Paul's request, but it placed him in a quandary. He had not understood the Jews; what charges was he to prefer against Paul when he was sent to Rome? Fortunately for Festus, King Agrippa came to Caesarea to pay his respects and as the king was a Jew, Festus asked him to hear Paul. Agrippa consented and the next day when he appeared before them, Paul gave his greatest and last recorded defense. He told of his rearing as a Jew and of his faith in the coming of a Messiah: how he had persecuted the followers of Jesus and of his conversion on the Damascus road:

> "Wherefore, O King Agrippa, I was not disobedient to the heavenly vision, but declared first to those at Damascus, then at Jerusalem and throughout all the country of Judea, and also to the Gentiles, that they should repent and turn to God and perform deeds worthy of their repentance" (Acts 26:19, 20).

For this, he said, the Jews sought to kill him, even though their scriptures foretold that Christ would suffer and rise again and afford salvation both to Jews and Gentiles.

Festus could not understand these spiritual ideas and interrupted Paul's speech: "Paul, you are mad; your great learning is turning you mad" (Acts

26:24). The apostle denied this, and turning to Agrippa, said, "Do you believe the prophets? I know that you believe" (Acts 26:27). Agrippa answered, "In a short time you think to make me a Christian!" (Acts 26:28).

Festus signifies "the transient joys of the external life," and the name *Agrippa* means "one who causes pain at birth." Of the reaction of these two states of consciousness to Truth, Charles Fillmore says:

> So long as we are enjoying ourselves in the sense life, our ears are usually dull to Truth: Festus was not moved by Paul's eloquent appeal. But pain brings us very close to an acceptance of the higher way: Agrippa was almost persuaded to believe (MD 29).

We are prone to consider pain as wholly undesirable and contrary to God's will. Certainly He never inflicts suffering upon us as punishment for our misdeeds. We bring it upon ourself by our violation of His law. Yet pain serves a purpose, for it often furnishes the incentive to turn to God and our life is enriched immeasurably. In recognition of this Jesus said we are blessed when we mourn for through sorrow (not by it) we find comfort in our Lord. In this case Agrippa was not yet receptive to the whole Truth but Paul's words affected him to some degree. It was undoubtedly his verdict that influenced Festus to agree that Paul had done nothing worthy of imprisonment or death and could have been freed had he not already appealed to Caesar.

To human judgment it seems that Paul made a

mistake in seeking redress from the Roman emperor, but when one's true motive and wholehearted purpose is to serve the Lord Jesus Christ, there are no mistakes. To go to Rome had long been Paul's ardent desire, and he had planned to do so since the time he wrote the epistle to the Romans. Moreover, the Lord had revealed to him, "you must bear witness also at Rome" (Acts 23:11). Surely it was no part of Paul's wish to enter the city as a prisoner. It is not always given to us to dictate the outer form the fulfillment of our desire will take. But if we will trust God and see the good in each experience, be it pleasant or otherwise, the realization is bound to come that every happening is a stepping-stone to our goal, every condition a part of the best plan for us at the moment.

The fact that Paul met imprisonment in the most constructive manner and rendered an outstanding service to the Christian cause while in Rome indicates that his sojourn there must have been a blessing to him as it has been to untold generations of those who love Jesus Christ.

Paul in Rome

Acts 27–31
Ephesians, Philippians, Colossians, Philemon,
I Timothy, Titus, II Timothy

At last Paul was on his way to Rome, accompanied by Luke and Aristarchus. They embarked on an Asiatic coastal vessel in charge of a Roman centurion, named Julius, and a small body of soldiers. The record of this journey is given in the 27th and 28th chapters of Acts, and is acknowledged to be one of the most valuable documents in existence concerning the seamanship of ancient times. It is also a priceless record of Paul's life, for it shows his spiritual wisdom and strength in a crisis.

Sailing north and then west of Cyprus, they reached Myra in Lycia and transferred to an Alexandrian grain ship for Italy. By October they reached Crete, at a time when navigation was becoming dangerous. Paul's advice that it was unwise to continue the journey was rejected.

The ship had barely set out from Crete when the wind, the northeaster, shifted to the north and drove it out to sea. For fourteen days the storm continued. Fear and despair took possession of the entire company with the exception of Paul. Standing forth in the midst of them he said:

I now bid you take heart; for there will be no loss of life among you, but only of the ship. For this very night there stood by me an angel of the God to whom I belong and whom I worship, and he said, "Do not be afraid, Paul; you must stand before Caesar; and lo, God has granted you all those who sail with you." So take heart, men, for I have faith in God that it will be exactly as I have been told (Acts 27:22-25).

When we are close to God our confidence in His power to preserve is greater than our fear of danger. His protecting Presence is always at hand, but if our mind is obsessed by the destructive emotion of fear, we do not realize this. If we will listen to the word of Truth (Paul), our fears are dispelled and we are protected against any disaster that may threaten us.

At length the vessel grounded and the entire company of two hundred and seventy-six (or seventy-six, according to other ancient authorities) landed on the island of Malta. There the people showed them kindness, making a fire and giving them food:

Paul had gathered a bundle of sticks and put them on the fire, when a viper came out because of the heat and fastened on his hand. When the natives saw the creature hanging from his hand, they said to one another, "No doubt this man is a murderer. Though he has escaped from the sea, justice has not allowed him to live." He, however, shook off the creature into the fire and suffered no harm. They waited, expecting him to swell up or suddenly fall down dead; but when they had waited a long time and saw no misfortune come to him, they changed their minds and said that he was a god (Acts 28:3-6).

We are not subject to the things that are usually injurious if we have faith in God. All life is divine in whatever form it manifests, and we experience dire results only so long as we are in bondage to the race thought that certain things are poisonous. When we rise above this erroneous belief and perceive God's life in every creature, we cannot be harmed by it. This incident recalls Jesus' promise to His followers, "They will pick up serpents, and if they drink any deadly thing, it will not hurt them" (Mark 16:18).

As Paul had shown himself to be an extraordinary person, he was taken to the island's chief, whose name was Publius. He entertained the apostle and his companions for three days. The father of Publius was ill with a fever, and Paul "prayed, and putting his hands on him healed him" (Acts 28:8). Then other sick folk came and were also healed. Mighty is the word of Truth!

Three months later the shipwrecked men sailed on another ship, provided with all that they needed for the journey to Italy. When they landed at Puteoli, the port of Rome, Paul and his friends were warmly greeted by the Christians of that city. As they approached Rome, a delegation from the church came out to meet him, and on seeing them "Paul thanked God and took courage" (Acts 28:15).

Of the spiritual significance of Paul's confinement in Rome, Charles Fillmore says:

Rome represents the head, in contrast to Jerusalem, which represents the heart. The head is the seat of the

dominating personal will, and also of the intellect in
man; to the outer man these are the seat of all strength
and power. . . .

Paul represents the divine word; Rome is the center
from which the will rules. When the will, guided by
sense intellect and the personal idea of ruling power,
imprisons the word, binds it in the realm of personal
understanding and dictatorship, the activity of Spirit
seems inhibited (MD 561).

The apostle was to remain a prisoner in the capital
city for two years. As in Caesarea, in Rome also Paul
was treated with unusual consideration. He was permitted to rent a house of his own and paid his
expenses, probably with monetary gifts from his
churches and friends. Though a Roman soldier was
constantly in attendance, Paul's house became a
meeting place for Christians. Shortly after his arrival
he held a conference with representatives of the Jews
and was asked to speak concerning his faith. He did
this and, though some Jews believed, the majority
did not, and the apostle again confined his preaching
to Gentiles, even converting some of the Roman
soldiers who guarded him.

Paul's life was a busy one, "preaching the kingdom of God and teaching about the Lord Jesus
Christ quite openly and unhindered" (Acts 28:31).
Several of his disciples and co-workers visited him,
among them Timothy, Luke, John Mark, and Aristarchus. During these years he wrote the epistles to
the Ephesians, Philippians, Colossians, and to
Philemon. As the order of their writing is unknown,
they are given here as listed in the Bible.

These "Letters of the Imprisonment" show the depths of Paul's spiritual realization. Several years had elapsed since he wrote the Epistle to the Romans, and he had passed through many experiences. They had been difficult ones but Paul had culled great lessons therefrom, and many of these he passed on to us in these four remarkable letters.

Ephesians

The authorship of Ephesians has been questioned. Some authorities are of the opinion that an unknown writer, borrowing from Paul's writings, wrote it as an introduction to the first published collection of Paul's writings. Unlike most of Paul's epistles, Ephesians does not deal with local conditions in the church but, like Romans, is more general in its teaching. It lacks the usual salutation and there are no personal references to anyone connected with the church, although Paul had spent almost three years in Ephesus and must have been well acquainted with various members. Bible scholars are of the opinion that it was not written to Ephesus exclusively but was intended as a circular letter to the churches in Asia Minor.

The general theme is the glory of the church as revealing God's purpose expressed in Christ Jesus. The church, the writer says, is grounded in Him (Eph. 1:4-14). Racial distinctions between Jews and Gentiles (a big issue in that day) do not matter to those who are "in Christ" (Eph. 2:10-15). The love of Christ Jesus is our salvation, and he prays:

> That according to the riches of his glory he may
> grant you to be strengthened with might through his
> Spirit in the inner man, and that Christ may dwell in
> your hearts through faith; that you, being rooted and
> grounded in love, may have power to comprehend with
> all the saints what is the breadth and length and height
> and depth, and to know the love of Christ which
> surpasses knowledge, that you may be filled with the
> fulness of God (Eph. 3:16-19).

The writer sees the church as the mystical body of
Christ and every believer shares in its high destiny.
He calls on all to enter into the unity of the Spirit
and thus contribute to the good of the whole:

> I therefore, a prisoner for the Lord, beg you to lead a
> life worthy of the calling to which you have been
> called, with all lowliness and meekness, with patience,
> forbearing one another in love, eager to maintain the
> unity of the Spirit in the bond of peace. There is one
> body and one Spirit, just as you were called to the one
> hope that belongs to your call, one Lord, one faith, one
> baptism, one God and Father of us all, who is above all
> and through all and in all (Eph. 4:1-6).

He insists that there must be a clear distinction
between the morals of the Christian and those of the
unbeliever (Eph. 4:17-24).

Beginning with Chapter 4:25 to 5:21, the subject
matter concerns Christian ethics. We are cautioned
to shun the flagrant sins of the unbeliever and called
upon to love as Christ Jesus loves, even to the point
of sacrifice. We need no longer walk in darkness for

we are children of light:

"Awake, O sleeper, and arise from the dead,
   and Christ shall give you light"

(Eph. 5:14).

Christian behavior in the home is the subject covered from Chapter 5:22 to 6:9.

The letter rises to a climax as the writer urges us to clothe ourselves in the armor of God:

Be strong in the Lord and in the strength of his might. Put on the whole armor of God, that you may be able to stand against the wiles of the devil (Eph. 6:10, 11).

Philippians

Philippi was the first European city Paul visited. There he and Silas had been put in prison and made their remarkable escape (Acts 16:25-34). This epistle is sometimes referred to as Paul's "love letter" for, with the exception of Philemon and II Timothy, it is the most personal of his writings and shows his deep affection for the Macedonian church.

This church had been most considerate of Paul and Epaphroditus had recently brought him a gift of money from them. Paul was writing to express his appreciation of their generosity and to give news of himself. He is torn between the desire to "depart and be with Christ" (Phil. 1:23), and the need he feels to continue his ministry among the followers of Jesus

Christ (Phil. 1:24-26).

Paul admonishes them to have "this mind among yourselves, which you have in Christ Jesus" (Phil. 2:5), who, though He knew himself to be one with God, was willing to take on the limitations of man and suffer death. Because of His humility, God exalted Him and "bestowed on him the name which is above every name, that at the name of Jesus every knee should bow . . . and every tongue confess that Jesus Christ is Lord, to the glory of God the Father" (Phil. 2:9-11).

The apostle warns against those who are trying to bring Gentile converts under the Mosaic Law. At one time he himself had been proud of his Jewish heritage, but now he is willing to put all behind him for a greater goal.

> Indeed I count everything as loss because of the surpassing worth of knowing Christ Jesus my Lord. For his sake I have suffered the loss of all things, and count them as refuse, in order that I may gain Christ (Phil. 3:8).

"Stand firm . . . in the Lord" (Phil. 4:1), he says, and urges them to follow the example he set them that they may find the peace of God (Phil. 4:9). Despite his imprisonment Paul rejoices in the Lord greatly:

> I have learned, in whatever state I am, to be content. I know how to abound; in any and all circumstances I have learned the secret of facing plenty and hunger,

abundance and want. I can do all things in him who
strengthens me (Eph. 4:11-13).

Surely this is one of the greatest lessons anyone
can learn. Our state of mind is usually governed by
outer circumstances. We are happy when things are
pleasant, miserable when they are not. "Do not
judge by appearances, but judge with right judgment" (John 7:24), Jesus tells us. Wisdom reveals
that God is everywhere evenly present and that we
can find Him in even the most unhappy experiences
if we seek. Always, "Closer is He than breathing, and
nearer than hands and feet," and to realize this and
remain unaffected by conditions is Christ mastery.

Colossians

Colossae was a city in Asia Minor, some hundred
miles from Ephesus. The church had been founded
by one of Paul's disciples, probably Epaphras, but
Paul had never visited it. Epaphras came to see Paul
in Rome and brought the disturbing news that the
Christ message was being adulterated by Gnosticism,
a combination of Greek philosophy and Oriental
mysticism.

Gnosticism comes from the Greek word *gnosis,*
which means "knowledge" (but not as the word is
commonly understood now). Its knowledge was a
sort of supernatural wisdom by which it was claimed
that its followers were brought to a true understanding of the universe and saved from the evil world of
matter. Gnosticism taught that the world creator

was not the spiritual God revealed in the Jewish Old Testament, but that from Him came various beings in a descending scale of value, the lowest of which was the imperfect being called the "Demiurge." The teaching was intellectually exclusive, insisting that spiritual enlightenment was limited to those who were given a secret instruction by special teachers, and who performed the prescribed rites. The Eleusinian mysteries and Mithraism, both of which contained Gnostic elements, were two of the most popular religions of the day.

When Paul wrote to the Colossians, Gnosticism was beginning to creep into the Christian church. Its influence was to increase in later years, and by the time some of the General Epistles were written, Gnosticism had become a full-fledged heresy to be vigorously attacked.

Paul warned the Colossians against what he believed to be a dangerous menace, and endeavored to put them on the right track again. "Be not deceived," he said repeatedly in substance.

The epistle is Christcentric, emphasizing throughout the supremacy of Christ Jesus:

> He is the image of the invisible God, the first-born of all creation; for in him all things were created, in heaven and on earth, visible and invisible, whether thrones or dominions or principalities or authorities—all things were created through him and for him. He is before all things, and in him all things hold together. He is the head of the body, the church; he is the beginning, the first-born from the dead, that in everything he might be pre-eminent. For in him all the fulness of God was

pleased to dwell, and through him to reconcile to himself all things, whether on earth or in heaven, making peace by the blood of his cross (Col. 1:15-20).

From the Christian point of view, Gnosticism promulgated three main errors:

(1) It held that only a few who were selected for the secret teaching could achieve salvation. Paul's position is that perfection is attainable by all in Christ Jesus, "Him we proclaim, warning every man and teaching every man in all wisdom, that we may present every man mature [perfect] in Christ" (Col. 1:28).

(2) It believed that the universe contained a number of beings of various degrees of power and importance ranging from the Demiurge to God, and that Jesus Christ was only one of the superior beings. Paul refutes this by the unequivocal declaration, "In him the whole fulness of deity dwells bodily" (Col. 2:9).

(3) Gnosticism taught angel-worship and an extreme asceticism. Paul utterly rejects the former, declaring that Christ should be the only and supreme object of worship for He is the creator of angels and head of the church (Col. 2:18). True asceticism is abstaining from evil thoughts and passions (Col. 3:5-11). We should express the spiritual virtues that come from a union with Christ:

Put on then, as God's chosen ones, holy and beloved,

compassion, kindness, lowliness, meekness, and patience, forbearing one another and, if one has a complaint against another, forgiving each other; as the Lord has forgiven you, so you also must forgive. And above all these put on love, which binds everything together in perfect harmony. And let the peace of Christ rule in your hearts, to which indeed you were called in the one body. And be thankful (Col. 3:12-15).

The remainder of the letter takes up the theme of manifesting the Christ Spirit in domestic relations (Col. 3:18–4:1), and ends with admonitions to pray.

Philemon

This is the shortest of Paul's letters and the only one written about a strictly personal matter. Though Philemon was a member of the church at Colossae, he had probably contacted Paul in Ephesus and knew him well. Philemon was evidently a man of means for he owned slaves, one of whom, Onesimus, had perhaps stolen from him and run away. Somehow Onesimus came in contact with Paul in Rome and was converted. The apostle, realizing Philemon's rights, persuaded the runaway slave to return to his master, and sent this letter with him.

After a warm and loving greeting to Philemon, Paul reveals his purpose in writing. He speaks of Onesimus as "my child" and says he would like to keep him, "in order that he might serve me on your behalf during my imprisonment for the gospel" (Philem.

1:13). He asks Philemon to receive Onesimus kindly and treat him as a brother rather than a servant (Philem. 1:16, 17). Also Paul offers to assume any loss suffered by Philemon at the hands of his slave (Philem. 1:18). He hints that Onesimus could be sent back to Rome to make himself useful to Paul in prison (Philem. 1:21).

This epistle expresses to the fullest the apostle's compassionate spirit.

The Book of Acts ends abruptly with Paul as a prisoner in Rome. One theory, based on tradition, says that he was acquitted after two years and resumed his missionary journeys. The Pastoral Epistles mention his presence in Macedonia, Nicopolis, Troas, Corinth, and Miletus. On some unknown charge, probably as a disturber of the peace, he was again arrested and returned to Rome. During this period Paul wrote I and II Timothy and Titus. It was no mild imprisonment this second time, as shown in II Timothy.

The other theory, held by some modern scholars, is that Paul did not write the Pastoral Epistles. Their opinion is that these deal with conditions that developed in the church a number of years after Paul's death. They also call attention to the fact that the style of writing is unlike that of the apostle's earlier letters, and they assign the second century as the possible date of their writing. All agree, however, that the spirit of them is Paul's.

As we read the three epistles we are struck with the difference in subject matter between them and Paul's other letters. The name *Pastoral* was given them because they contain instructions to pastors or those in charge of churches. The time had come when it was necessary for Paul to turn his work over to others, and these letters deal largely with the practical side of church organization and administration. The church was the channel through which the Christ message was to be disseminated and it needed well-trained leaders who were not only capable of giving a "sound" teaching, as Paul insisted on, but also were able to instruct other teachers, maintain discipline among the members, and oversee the entire functioning of the church. This was no small order, and one feels Paul's earnest plea to keep the Christ Spirit alive through an effectively managed human institution.

I Timothy

Timothy was Paul's special protégé and had proved himself to be a loyal "son" and a faithful worker on many occasions during the missionary journeys. Paul had left him in charge of the church at Ephesus.

The letter begins with the apostle's advice to Timothy to restrain certain members in the church who are insisting on teaching but are not sufficiently trained, and are discussing subjects that are irrelevant and contrary to the Christ message. Timothy is to hold to the sound doctrine which he had learned from Paul.

The Gospel is universal, Paul maintains, and the church should pray for all people. "This is good and it is acceptable in the sight of God our Savior" (I Tim. 2:3). However, to be effective, prayer must be reinforced by clean and holy living. Women are cautioned against ostentation. It is, rather, godliness of character that best becomes them (I Tim. 2:8-15). Paul thinks that a woman's greatest service lies in the field of being wife and mother.

Then come specific qualifications for church leaders, namely bishops and deacons. Surely these apply to all ministers for all time:

> If any one aspires to the office of bishop, he desires a noble task. Now a bishop must be above reproach, the husband of one wife, temperate, sensible, dignified, hospitable, an apt teacher, no drunkard, not violent but gentle, not quarrelsome, and no lover of money. He must manage his own household well, keeping his children submissive and respectful in every way; for if a man does not know how to manage his own household, how can he care for God's church? He must not be a recent convert, or he may be puffed up with conceit and fall into the condemnation of the devil; moreover he must be well thought of by outsiders, or he may fall into reproach and the snare of the devil.
> Deacons likewise must be serious, not double-tongued, not addicted to much wine, not greedy for gain; they must hold the mystery of the faith with a clear conscience (I Tim. 3:1-9).

Timothy is cautioned against those who are leaning toward ascetic practices. Paul considers this an emphasis upon the wrong things (I Tim. 4:1-5). As a good minister Timothy will be faithful to his trust by holding the Christ ideal before the church members constantly. He should keep his own faith fresh and strong, and "set the believers an example in speech and conduct, in love, in faith, in purity" (I Tim. 4:12).

The handling of special cases is the subject of Chapter 5 to 6:2. Paul says to exhort rather than rebuke older members, see that elderly and needy widows are cared for (but he advises young widows to remarry), and be cautious about restoring an offending member to office in the church.

The apostle then returns to the subject of teachers who are driven by ambition and greed, "imagining that godliness is a means of gain" (I Tim. 6:5):

> For the love of money is the root of all evils; it is through this craving that some have wandered away from the faith and pierced their hearts with many pangs (I Tim. 6:10).

The closing word to Timothy is an entreaty to guard as a sacred trust the opportunity given him to serve the church as a true minister of Jesus Christ.

Titus

Titus, a Greek converted by Paul, played an important part in his ministry. Though he is not mentioned in the Book of Acts, Paul speaks of him several times in his letters. At the Jerusalem Conference, Titus was a strong point in Paul's favor for, as a Gentile, he had not submitted to all the practices of Judaism, and yet, obviously, he was a worthy Christian. When matters were critical in Corinth, Paul sent Titus as his delegate, showing that he considered him capable and trustworthy. Titus had been placed in charge of the church in Crete, though it is not known when this church was founded.

There was not the close personal affection between Paul and Titus that there was between Paul and Timothy, and the letter to Titus is more formal and official. The instructions and advice are similar, in substance, to those given in the first epistle to Timothy. The apostle again deals with proper qualifications for church officials, the manner in which erroneous teachings should be handled, and the deportment of Titus himself as a Christian minister.

It was probably in A.D. 64 or 65 that Paul was again taken prisoner by the Roman government. The situation was very different from his first confinement in Rome. Paul was now awaiting execution. Under these trying circumstances Paul wrote his second epistle to Timothy. It is likely that later both Paul and Peter met their death at the command of Nero.

II Timothy

This is a beautiful letter, filled with such courage and faith that it has been an inspiration to Christians throughout the ages. It is very personal. Paul calls Timothy his "beloved child," thanks God for his faithfulness, and longs to see him once more (II Tim. 1:1-5). He appeals to Timothy to keep the gift of grace which God bestowed upon him when he was consecrated for service. He must never be ashamed that he is a Christian, nor ashamed of Paul who is even now imprisoned for his faith. Rather let him be ready to suffer shame, if need be, for God will give him strength (II Tim. 1:16-18).

Knowing that his days of preaching are over, the apostle urges Timothy to continue his (Paul's) work. Though Paul himself is in prison as a common criminal, this must not stop the spread of the Gospel. Timothy is to be the kind of servant that God will approve:

> Do your best to present yourself to God as one approved, a workman who has no need to be ashamed, rightly handling the word of truth (II Tim. 2:15).

Timothy is charged to "preach the word, be urgent in season and out of season, convince, rebuke, and exhort, be unfailing in patience and in teaching" (II Tim. 4:2). Others may depart from the Gospel, for its ideals are exacting and they will seek an easier way, but Timothy is to remain staunch, do the work of an evangelist and fulfill his ministry. Paul knows that the time of his departure is near at hand but, he says:

> I have fought the good fight, I have finished the race, I have kept the faith. Henceforth there is laid up for me the crown of righteousness, which the Lord, the righteous judge, will award to me on that Day, and not only to me but also to all who have loved his appearing (II Tim. 4:7, 8).

He asks Timothy to come to him as soon as possible and bring the cloak he left at Troas, and also his books and parchments.

Release was soon to come. In his book, "The Life of St. Paul," James Stalker writes the following of Paul's appearance at Nero's court:

> On the judgment-seat, clad in the imperial purple, sat a man who in a bad world had attained the eminence of being the very worst and meanest being in it—a man stained with every crime, the murderer of his own mother, of his wives and of his best benefactors . . . and in the prisoner's dock stood the best man the world contained, his hair whitened with labors for the good of men and the glory of God.

Tradition states that Paul, as a Roman citizen, was executed by the sword. The story goes that when his head was struck it bounded thrice and each time it smote the ground a living fountain gushed forth, possessing a healing virtue and called the "healing waters." A church was later built at the supposed site. Paul's body was thrown into the criminals' charnel house but it was claimed by a lady named Lucina, a Roman convert, and buried in her own garden.

The dauntless spirit that was Paul's marches on. Through the Paul in us, our will becomes united with God's will and we speak the word of Truth with authority and faith. And some day we shall know, as truly as did the great apostle, that our life "is hid with Christ in God" (Col. 3:3).

Messages from Paul's Epistles

As we study the wonderful truths given in the Pauline Epistles, we should keep in mind that Paul does not express the Christ consciousness fully. Only Jesus did that. As a person, Paul was one of the most advanced teachers the world has ever known and probably the foremost Christian preacher, but he was not the Savior and never considered himself the final authority. To him Jesus Christ was all in all. He did not want men to follow him, and he always held up to them the glory of Christ. His was the difficult task of giving the first interpretation of the Christ message, principally to the Gentile world. This he did supremely well and since his time the Christian religion has been filled with quotations from his epistles.

Paul is an essential link in the chain of spiritual development leading to the Christ consciousness. The way he persisted in his work is symbolic of the way we should persist in faithfully speaking the word of Truth to convert our own unregenerate states of consciousness. And even as Paul's love for Jesus Christ and steadfastness in declaring His message bore fruit, not only to himself but to all who heard his teaching, so does our love and faithfulness bear fruit also. The struggles we have, even the times of suffering and seeming defeat, are replicas of Paul's efforts to turn men to Christ and inspire them to live the Christ life.

The spoken words of Paul have been lost, except those recorded in The Acts, but his written words as given in his thirteen epistles are so rich in spirituality that we thank God that occasions arose which made it necessary for him to communicate with the churches. Because the members were human beings they had problems to meet, and Paul wrote to help them although, undoubtedly, he would rather have talked with them. What seemed a limitation to Paul has proved to be a blessing to each generation since his time.

In reading his letters it should be kept in mind that many portions deal with local conditions in the early Christian churches and, therefore, much of what he wrote has little application to our life. The Revised Standard Version of the Bible does much to clarify many passages. Paul often dictated his letters and as he was a very busy man and more intent on communicating an idea than in grammatical construction, his meaning is sometimes obscure. A good commentary, such as the Abingdon Bible Commentary, will also prove helpful. It is well to remember that the illumined intellect is the forerunner of spiritual realization. Unless our mind can grasp the sense of a passage, our interpretation of its spiritual meaning is neither consistent nor satisfying.

From the many profound truths given by Paul, twelve general subjects have been selected for this chapter, and quotations substantiating them taken from his letters. These quotations are all familiar and build up into a spiritual teaching that is intelligible and concise. They bring greater understanding, a deeper realization of the Jesus Christ presence, and encourage us to apply spiritual principles to everyday living.

1. The basis of Paul's theology is, obviously, the manifestation of God, the Father, in Jesus Christ, the Son, who is the Savior, the Redeemer, the Paraclete. "Christ is all, and in all" (Col. 3:11). This is so obvious that it need not be elaborated upon. We may begin, therefore, with Paul's concept of the innate divinity of man. This is a belief not generally accepted in Christian theology. Man is considered a sinner by nature. Man as primarily a divine being is the concept of Truth students. Jesus taught this ("You are the light of the world") and Paul expands it:

> I became a minister according to the divine office which was given to me for you, to make the word of God fully known, the mystery hidden for ages and generations but now made manifest to his saints. To them God chose to make known how great among the Gentiles are the riches of the glory of this mystery, which is Christ in you, the hope of glory (Col. 1:25-27).

> Do you not know that you are God's temple and that God's Spirit dwells in you? (I Cor. 3:16).

> It is the Spirit himself bearing witness with our spirit that we are children of God, and if children, then heirs, heirs of God and fellow heirs with Christ, provided we suffer with him in order that we may also be glorified with him (Rom. 8:16, 17).

2. When we accept the Truth that we are spiritual in nature and that the Christ who indwells us is our true self, we naturally ask why we have not expressed what we are in reality, the whole and perfect child of God. Paul answers by explaining that we have all been governed by the human mentality, which he refers to as the flesh, the carnal mind, and Adam. He urges us to free ourself of entanglement with our lower self:

> But I say, walk by the Spirit, and do not gratify the desires of the flesh. For the desires of the flesh are against the Spirit, and the desires of the Spirit are against the flesh; for these are opposed to each other, to prevent you from doing what you would. But if you are led by the Spirit you are not under the law. Now the works of the flesh are plain: immorality, impurity, licentiousness, idolatry, sorcery, enmity, strife, jealousy, anger, selfishness, dissension, party spirit, envy, drunkenness, carousing, and the like. I warn you, as I warned you before, that those who do such things shall not inherit the kingdom of God. But the fruit of the Spirit is love, joy, peace, patience, kindness, goodness, faithfulness, gentleness, self-control; against such there is no law. And those who belong to Christ Jesus have crucified the flesh with its passions and desires (Gal. 5:16-24).

> For as by a man came death, by a man has come also the resurrection of the dead. For as in Adam all die, so also in Christ shall all be made alive (I Cor. 15:21, 22).

> To set the mind on the flesh is death, but to set the mind on the Spirit is life and peace. For the mind that is set on the flesh is hostile to God; it does not submit to

God's law, indeed it cannot; and those who are in the
flesh cannot please God (Rom. 8:6-8).

3. We wonder whether it is possible for us to comprehend the great truths pertaining to God and our
relationship to Him. Paul's answer is "no" and
"yes." He says it is impossible for the mind of the
flesh, or the human mentality, to comprehend, but it
is possible for the indwelling Christ to reveal the
mystery of Godliness.

> "But it is the spirit in a man,
>> the breath of the Almighty that makes him
>> understand"
>
> *(Job 32:8).*

Paul reiterates this, in substance, explaining that,
because of His Spirit within us, we are capable of
discerning the things that belong to the spiritual
realm:

> God has revealed to us through the Spirit. For the
> Spirit searches everything, even the depths of God. For
> what person knows a man's thoughts except the spirit
> of the man which is in him? So also no one compre-
> hends the thoughts of God except the Spirit of God.
> Now we have received not the spirit of the world, but
> the Spirit which is from God, that we might understand
> the gifts bestowed on us by God. And we impart this in
> words not taught by human wisdom but taught by the
> Spirit, interpreting spiritual truths to those who possess
> the Spirit. The unspiritual man does not receive the
> gifts of the Spirit of God, for they are folly to him, and
> he is not able to understand them because they are
> spiritually discerned (I Cor. 2:10-14).

"For who has known the mind of the Lord so as to instruct him?" But we have the mind of Christ (I Cor. 2:16).

4. Faith in Christ is fundamental to the spiritual unfoldment to which we aspire. Through faith we become unified with anything. If our faith is given to the things of the material world we receive only the limited good to be derived therefrom. If our faith is centered in Christ the doors of the kingdom of heaven are opened to us. Paul insists that justification, redemption, salvation can come only as we are unified with Christ through faith, and he bids us exercise this God-given faculty.

For by grace you have been saved through faith; and this is not your own doing, it is the gift of God—not because of works, lest any man should boast (Eph. 2:8, 9).

As therefore you received Christ Jesus the Lord, so live in him, rooted and built up in him and established in the faith, just as you were taught, abounding in thanksgiving (Col. 2:6, 7).

Stand therefore, having girded your loins with truth, and having put on the breastplate of righteousness, and having shod your feet with the equipment of the gospel of peace; above all taking the shield of faith, with which you can quench all the flaming darts of the evil one (Eph. 6:14-16).

Fight the good fight of the faith; take hold of the eternal life to which you were called when you made

the good confession in the presence of many witnesses
(I Tim. 6:12).

5. The principle of "like attracts like" operates on
all levels of life. We become like that to which we
give our attention. Paul cautions us to guard against
the beliefs and opinions of those who are unawak-
ened spiritually for they are still governed by the
mind of the flesh, mortal consciousness. We no
longer have any congeniality with these when we are
endeavoring to develop our spiritual nature.
Although we are not to draw away from people, we
should be careful not to take on their destructive
states of consciousness:

Do not be mismated with unbelievers. For what part-
nership have righteousness and iniquity? Or what fellowship has light with darkness? What accord has Christ
with Belial? Or what has a believer in common with an
unbeliever? What agreement has the temple of God
with idols? For we are the temple of the living God; as
God said,

"I will live in them and move among them,
and I will be their God,
and they shall be my people.
Therefore come out from them,
and be separate from them, says the Lord,
and touch nothing unclean;
then I will welcome you"

(II Cor. 6:14-17).

See to it that no one makes a prey of you by philosophy and empty deceit, according to human tradition,
according to the elemental spirits of the universe, and
not according to Christ. For in him the whole fulness of

deity dwells bodily, and you have come to fulness of
life in him, who is the head of all rule and authority
(Col. 2:8-10).

6. Our aim is to quicken the Christ Mind, and to
do this requires that we look to Him and sustain the
upward vision. The instruction is,

> Turn to me and be saved,
>   all the ends of the earth!
>   For I am God, and there is no other"
>
> *(Isa. 45:22).*

This is the only valid guide. Paul expands this
instruction by telling us to love Him, behold Him,
and let our consciousness be filled with the things
that belong to His world:

> Set your minds on things that are above, not on
> things that are on earth. For you have died, and your
> life is hid with Christ in God (Col. 3:2, 3).

> Let the word of Christ dwell in you richly, as you
> teach and admonish one another in all wisdom, and as
> you sing psalms and hymns and spiritual songs with
> thankfulness in your hearts to God (Col. 3:16).

> And we all, with unveiled face, beholding the glory
> of the Lord, are being changed into his likeness from
> one degree of glory to another; for this comes from the
> Lord who is the Spirit (II Cor. 3:18).

> Finally brethren, whatever is true, whatever is hon-
> orable, whatever is just, whatever is pure, whatever is
> lovely, whatever is gracious, if there is any excellence, if

there is anything worthy of praise, think about these
things. (Phil. 4:8).

The work of regeneration cannot come through
the personal self. When we consciously desire to
unify ourself with Him, our life is no longer ours but
His, and we may rest assured that He will not let us
out of His care and keeping:

> For God is at work in you, both to will and to work
> for his good pleasure (Phil. 2:13).
>
> And I am sure that he who began a good work in you
> will bring it to completion at the day of Jesus Christ
> (Phil. 1:6).
>
> I know whom I have believed, and I am sure that he is
> able to guard until that Day what has been entrusted to
> me (II Tim. 1:12).

7. Discipline is one of the most unpopular and yet
one of the most necessary words in our language. It
means "control gained by enforcing obedience or
order," and without discipline we cannot be successful in any endeavor. This is easily understood when
applied to accomplishment in the world. The
successful artist, musician, scientist, or businessman
is the one who is willing to train in his chosen field.

As regards spiritual development, discipline
means the control of our mind and emotions. This is
requisite if we are to obey the spiritual rules. We
cannot permit ourself to think destructively or give
way to negative emotions, and, at the same time,

comply with the provisions of God's law. In Proverbs
we read:

> "He who is slow to anger is better than the
> mighty,
> and he who rules his spirit than he who takes a
> city"
>
> *(Prov. 16:32).*

The victory is to be won in ourself before our consciousness can become a channel for those divine
qualities that make for spiritual mastery. All great
teachers stress the necessity for self-discipline. Paul
is no exception and he outlines several methods for
gaining self-control:

> We destroy arguments and every proud obstacle to
> the knowledge of God, and take every thought captive
> to obey Christ (II Cor. 10:5).

> But if I build up again those things which I tore
> down, then I prove myself a transgressor (Gal. 2:18).

> Have no anxiety about anything, but in everything
> by prayer and supplication with thanksgiving let your
> requests be made known to God (Phil. 4:6).

> Whatever you do, in word or deed, do everything in
> the name of the Lord Jesus, giving thanks to God the
> Father through him (Col. 3:17).

> For freedom Christ has set us free; stand fast there-
> fore, and do not submit again to a yoke of slavery (Gal.
> 5:11).

> Do you not know that in a race all the runners compete, but only one receives the prize? So run that you may obtain it. Every athlete exercises self-control in all things. They do it to receive a perishable wreath, but we an imperishable (I Cor. 9:24, 25).

God's law governs the universe and the life of all creatures. We cannot disregard it with impunity. Persistence in spiritual discipline should be our watchword, and Christ has given us the capacity and strength to move steadily forward:

> Do not be deceived; God is not mocked, for whatever a man sows, that he will also reap. For he who sows to his own flesh will from the flesh reap corruption; but he who sows to the Spirit will from the Spirit reap eternal life. And let us not grow weary in well-doing, for in due season we shall reap, if we do not lose heart (Gal. 6:7-9).

> And if the bugle gives an indistinct sound, who will get ready for battle? (I Cor. 14:8).

> Hence I remind you to rekindle the gift of God that is within you through the laying on of my hands; for God did not give us a spirit of timidity but a spirit of power and love and self-control (II Tim. 1:6, 7).

8. Man is a spiritual being of Spirit, soul, and body. Therefore, our so-called physical organism is not a separate entity but derives from Spirit, and is dependent upon soul or consciousness for its functioning. It is essential that we have the right concept of our body as a sacred vessel, housing the Christ life

during our sojourn on earth. Paul repeatedly defines the true nature of the body. He urges respect for it and insists that it should not be subjected to abuse:

> Do you not know that your body is a temple of the Holy Spirit within you, which you have from God? You are not your own; you were bought with a price. So glorify God in your body (I Cor. 6:19, 20).

> It is sown a physical body, it is raised a spiritual body. If there is a physical body, there is also a spiritual body (I Cor. 15:44).

> So you also must consider yourselves dead to sin and alive to God in Christ Jesus. Let not sin therefore reign in your mortal bodies, to make you obey their passions (Rom. 6:11, 12).

> We know that the whole creation has been groaning in travail together until now; and not only the creation, but we ourselves, who have the first fruits of the Spirit, groan inwardly as we wait for adoption as sons, the redemption of our bodies (Rom. 8:22, 23).

> If the Spirit of him who raised Jesus from the dead dwells in you, he who raised Christ Jesus from the dead will give life to your mortal bodies also through his Spirit which dwells in you (Rom. 8:11).

9. Jesus said, "Blessed . . . are those who hear the word of God, and keep it!" (Luke 11:28). This is a never-ending challenge to the Truth student. Our mind can grasp an idea, accept it and declare it with great eloquence. Yet if our preaching is of one kind and our practice of another, the consciousness be-

comes a house divided against itself. Then words lose their potency and we wonder why we are unable to help either ourself or others. "Physician, heal yourself" is our first task:

> You then who teach others, will you not teach yourself? While you preach against stealing, do you steal? You who say that one must not commit adultery, do you commit adultery? You who abhor idols, do you rob temples? You who boast in the law, do you dishonor God by breaking the law? (Rom. 2:21-23).

> Take heed to yourself and to your teaching: hold to that, for by so doing you will save both yourself and your hearers (I Tim. 4:16).

Along with bringing to our attention the necessity of making our actions conform to our beliefs, Paul gives many instructions which, if studiously followed, will balance faith and works:

> Put off your old nature which belongs to your former manner of life and is corrupt through deceitful lusts, and be renewed in the spirit of your minds, and put on the new nature, created after the likeness of God in true righteousness and holiness.
> Therefore, putting away falsehood, let every one speak the truth with his neighbor, for we are members one of another. Be angry but do not sin; do not let the sun go down on your anger, and give no opportunity to the devil. Let the thief no longer steal, but rather let him labor, doing honest work with his hands, so that he may be able to give to those in need. Let no evil talk come out of your mouths, but only such as is good for edifying, as fits the occasion, that it may impart grace to those who hear. And do not grieve the Holy Spirit of

God, in whom you were sealed for the day of redemption. Let all bitterness and wrath and anger and clamor and slander be put away from you, with all malice, and be kind to one another, tenderhearted, forgiving one another, as God in Christ forgave you (Eph. 4:22-32).

So, whether you eat or drink, or whatever you do, do all to the glory of God (I Cor. 10:31).

10. The perfect definition of the Deity is given by John who says, "God is love" (I John 4:8). To understand this and to feel the great tenderness of the Father for His children provides much comfort and the incentive to walk the path that leads to the kingdom despite the many obstacles on our way. Nothing is too hard if we know we are loved and can love in return. Above all else Jesus portrays God as a loving Father, and Paul, who caught this vision, is also emphatic in declaring it: .

Who shall separate us from the love of Christ? Shall tribulation, or distress, or persecution, or famine, or nakedness, or peril, or sword? As it is written,

"For thy sake we are being killed all the day long;
we are regarded as sheep to be slaughtered."

No, in all these things we are more than conquerors through him who loved us. For I am sure that neither death, nor life, nor angels, nor principalities, nor things present, nor things to come, nor powers, nor height, nor depth, nor anything else in all creation, will be able to separate us from the love of God in Jesus Christ our Lord (Rom. 8:35-39).

But God, who is rich in mercy, out of the great love with which he loved us, even when we were dead through our trespasses, made us alive together with Christ (Eph. 2:4, 5).

But, as it is written,

"What no eye has seen, nor ear heard,
nor the heart of man conceived,
what God has prepared for those who love him"
(I Cor. 2:9).

As we are loved, so must we also love our Lord. And (what is sometimes much more difficult) we must love our fellow man:

Owe no one anything, except to love one another; for he who loves his neighbor has fulfilled the law. . . . Love does no wrong to a neighbor; therefore love is the fulfilling of the law (Rom. 13:8-10).

Let love be genuine; hate what is evil, hold fast to what is good; love one another with brotherly affection; outdo one another in showing honor (Rom. 12:9, 10).

For you were called to freedom, brethren; only do not use your freedom as an opportunity for the flesh, but through love be servants of one another (Gal. 5:13).

If I speak in the tongues of man and of angels, but have not love, I am a noisy gong or a clanging cymbal. . . . So faith, hope, love abide, these three; but the greatest of these is love (I Cor. 13:1-13).

11. Is the goal of spiritual unfoldment worth the

struggle to attain it? It is undoubtedly a "strait and narrow path" but it leads to the kingdom of God, or the conscious awareness of the presence of all-good. From this awareness there are released in us the attributes and powers of the Christ indwelling which enable us to go steadily forward. Each step helps us to forget the human struggle and enter more and more into the freedom and peace that comes of knowing our oneness with our Lord. As Paul says:

> There is therefore now no condemnation for those who are in Christ Jesus. For the law of the Spirit of life in Christ Jesus has set me free from the law of sin and death (Rom. 8:1, 2).

> But now we are discharged from the law, dead to that which held us captive, so that we serve not under the old written code but in the new life of the Spirit (Rom. 7:6).

> We know that in everything God works for good with those who love him, who are called according to his purpose. . . . What then shall we say to this? If God is for us, who is against us? (Rom. 8:28-31).

> Therefore, if any one is in Christ, he is a new creation; the old has passed away, behold, the new has come (II Cor. 5:17).

> Just as we have borne the image of the man of dust, we shall also bear the image of the man of heaven (I Cor. 15:49).

12. "Seek, and you will find" (Matt. 7:7) is the promise of Jesus. Yet our involvement in the inter-

ests and problems of life often tempts us to overlook
the fact that our part is to seek with one purpose in
view. "You shall have no other gods before me"
(Exod. 20:3) is the requirement that crowns our
search with success. With singleness of mind and a
whole heart, says Paul, we are to proceed in this great
adventure of the soul:

> Not that I have already obtained this or am already
> perfect; but I press on to make it my own, because
> Christ Jesus has made me his own. Brethren, I do not
> consider that I have made it my own; but one thing I
> do, forgetting what lies behind and straining forward to
> what lies ahead, I press on toward the goal for the prize
> of the upward call of God in Christ Jesus (Phil.
> 3:12-14).

Let us not procrastinate. There is no time but
now. The call has come and the blessed present is
here that we may answer Him:

> Besides this you know what hour it is, how it is full
> time now for you to wake from sleep. For salvation is
> nearer to us now than when we first believed: the night
> is far gone, the day is at hand. Let us then cast off the
> works of darkness and put on the armor of light (Rom.
> 13:11, 12).

> Behold, now is the acceptable time; behold, now is
> the day of salvation (II Cor. 6:2).

All that anyone could do to quicken man to the
realization of the Christ presence and make him
worthy of his rich heritage in God, Paul did. And as

we leave this great apostle to the Gentiles for the time being, let us bow our head to receive his benediction:

The grace of the Lord Jesus Christ and the love of God and the fellowship of the Holy Spirit be with you all (II Cor. 13:14).

General Epistles (I)

Hebrews and James

With the conclusion of Paul's ministry and the rapid growth of the Christian communities, various difficulties arose, and the remaining eight epistles give spiritual light on these. The Epistle to the Hebrews stands by itself and is followed by the seven General or Catholic Epistles, so-named because they were usually addressed to Christians in general. In the main they are sermons for instruction and encouragement rather than letters, and they gained wide circulation among the early Christians.

As Bible students we should know the background and the local situation these epistles deal with, yet we need to go much further. As practical Truth students, we are interested primarily in the spiritual teaching they give. What were the enlightened writers of these letters saying to us? So much, if we will but open our ears to hear! For example, The Letter to the Hebrews confirms our faith that Christ is our all-sufficiency in all things. This we accept in theory, yet we continue to ask our Lord to move people and conditions, thinking that therein is the solution to the problem. Contact with Him is the only solution. Hebrews helps us to have a better understanding of Christ and increases our faith which, in turn, opens up a fuller communication with the only source of good.

Hebrews

The question, "Who wrote it?" has never been answered. Due to some similarities to portions of Paul's letters his name became associated with it, but as early as the third century Bible scholars were certain Paul was not the author. It has been ascribed to Barnabas, Luke, Apollos, and others, though there has never been general agreement as to who penned what is considered to be one of the best books of the New Testament, both from a literary and a spiritual standpoint. Nor is it known where or when it was written. It is thought that the date of writing was the latter part of the first century.

The epistle was addressed to Hebrews or Jewish converts to Christianity. In many respects such converts had more to overcome than did Gentile converts. It was difficult for the former to reconcile the crucifixion of Jesus with their preconceived ideas of a Messiah who would conquer the world. Then too, Judaism offered an elaborate ritual which was absent in Christianity in its beginning. Even today some people find it easier to follow a prescribed form of religious observance than to adhere to a spiritual ideal which leaves much in the manner of worship to the discretion of the individual. The writer of Hebrews attempts to convince Jewish converts that the prophecies of the Old Testament were fulfilled in Jesus Christ. Thus he hopes to avert the danger of their return to Judaism or of falling short of complete faith in Jesus Christ. The key word of the epistle is "better." The good things of Judaism are merged into the better things of Christ:

> In many and various ways God spoke of old to our fathers by the prophets; but in these last days he has spoken to us by a Son, whom he appointed the heir of all things, through whom also he created the world (Heb. 1:1, 2).

Jesus Christ is above the prophets and angels (Heb. 1–2). He is superior to Moses (who was the servant of God), for He is the Son (Heb. 3–4). The generation that followed Moses out of Egypt did not enter into the Promised Land because of unbelief, and the writer of Hebrews warns, "Take care, brethren, lest there be in any of you an evil, unbelieving heart, leading you to fall away from the living God" (Heb. 3:12).

We are promised rest through our belief but we must be courageous in claiming it:

> So then, there remains a sabbath rest for the people of God . . . Let us therefore strive to enter that rest, that no one fall by the same sort of disobedience. For the word of God is living and active, sharper than any two-edged sword, piercing to the division of soul and spirit, of joints and marrow, and discerning the thoughts and intentions of the heart. . . . Let us then with confidence draw near to the throne of grace, that we may receive mercy and find grace to help in time of need (Heb. 4:9-16).

Chapters 5–8:6 develop the idea that Christianity represents recovery of the faith of Abraham before the giving of the law. From the time of Moses to that of Jesus Christ, the law had been gradually submerged under legalism and the Aaronic priesthood had degenerated. Faith was recovered in Jesus, who is described as a "high priest for ever after the order of Melchizedek" (Heb. 6:20).

Melchizedek was the king of Salem and priest of God Most High. Abraham brought tithes and offerings to him and received his blessing (Gen. 14:18-20). Melchizedek had no recorded "beginning of days nor end of life, but resembling the Son of God he continues a priest for ever" (Heb. 7:3). In other words, there was no genealogy concerning him, no priestly records such as were carefully kept of the high priests. Melchizedek symbolizes the ideal priest, a divine figure without human origin and existing eternally. In contrast, therefore, to the Levitical priests who are mortal men with a limited life span, Jesus Christ is an immortal priest whose work is permanent and continual:

> Consequently he is able for all time to save those who draw near to God through him, since he always lives to make intercession for them (Heb. 7:25).

Charles Fillmore says that Melchizedek signifies:

> The divine will established in man in righteousness, justice, and peace. . . . Melchizedek really represents the Christ Mind or superconsciousness, that which when ruling in man's consciousness establishes and

maintains right doing, perfect adjustment, peace, and perfection (MD 438).

Melchizedek is the Christ functioning in the spiritually awakened individual, opening the way for the Christed one as represented in Christ Jesus.

The writer maintains that through Jesus Christ a new covenant was established (Heb. 8:7-10). It is better than the old covenant, for Jesus Christ is superior to the Aaronic priests. The prophet Jeremiah had foretold a new covenant between God and man (Jer. 31:31-34), which had now been fulfilled:

> "This is the covenant that I will make with the house of
>   Israel
> after those days, says the Lord:
> I will put my laws into their minds,
> and write them on their hearts,
> and I will be their God,
> and they shall be my people.
> And they shall not teach every one his fellow
> or every one his brother, saying, 'Know the Lord,'
> for all shall know me,
> from the least of them to the greatest.
> For I will be merciful toward their iniquities,
> and I will remember their sins no more"
>   *(Heb. 8:10-12).*

By the sacrifice of His own life Jesus established the new covenant. His sacrifice is better than the many sacrifices made by the Jewish high priest. Once each year the high priest entered the Holy of Holies alone and made an offering to atone for the sins of all

the people. The Jews believed that a reconciliation
between God and man could come only through the
shedding of blood. But now the Jewish high priest
had been replaced by a greater One who offered the
perfect sacrifice once and for all time:

> Therefore he is the mediator of a new covenant, so
> that those who are called may receive the promised
> eternal inheritance, since a death has occurred which
> redeems them from the transgressions under the first
> covenant (Heb. 9:15).

The doctrine of the vicarious atonement made by
Jesus Christ is prominent in Christian theology; it is
accepted by Unity but interpreted differently.
Charles Fillmore states:

> The atonement as it has been understood by Chris-
> tian people in the past has not taken sin, suffering, and
> death from the world; therefore it must be that their
> understanding has fallen short of the Truth. Spiritual
> understanding of the atonement shows the way to
> deliverance from sin and consequently from all the
> effects of sin. In proportion as people understand and
> have faith in Jesus Christ as their actual Savior from sin,
> they are set free from appetite, passion, jealousy, preju-
> dice, and all selfishness; wholeness of mind and body is
> the result. The ultimate of this knowledge and of daily
> practice in overcoming (even as Jesus Himself over-
> came) will be a new race that will demonstrate eternal
> life—the lifting up of the whole man—spirit, soul, and
> body—into the Christ consciousness of oneness with
> the Father. By means of the atonement—reconcilia-
> tion, or at-one-ment—that Jesus Christ reestablished
> between God and man, we can regain our original estate

as sons of God, here upon earth. "Ye therefore shall be perfect, as your heavenly Father is perfect" (MD 79). (For additional information on the atonement see Chapter XIV in *Talks on Truth* by Charles Fillmore.)

The writer of Hebrews continues his argument that Christians need no longer accept the Jewish belief that, through their high priest, they enter the Holy of Holies once a year. Jesus, by His sacrifice, has opened for His followers "a new and living way" (Heb. 10:20) into the immediate presence of God. But we must come with sincere hearts, with faith, with a cleansed conscience, and having "our bodies washed with pure water" (Heb. 10:22), which probably refers to baptism. "Let us hold fast the confession of our hope without wavering, for he who promised is faithful" (Heb. 10:23).

There is a tendency on the part of some to drift away from the church because of the threat of persecution, and dire is the penalty for them. The followers of Christ should remember that the church has endured many things but has stood firm through them:

> Therefore do not throw away your confidence, which has a great reward. For you have need of endurance, so that you may do the will of God and receive what is promised (Heb. 10:35, 36).

This is a lesson for all to learn. Many times we actually do God's will and would receive His blessings but, lacking patience, we lapse into fear. This excludes the good that is already on its way to us. If

we are patient and confident, the reward that we
have earned will surely be made manifest.

The writer launches into a detailed account of the
superiority of the faith way in the most familiar and
best-loved chapter of his epistle, the eleventh:

> Now faith is assurance of things hoped for, the con-
> viction of things not seen (Heb. 11:1).

This is as fine a definition of faith as has ever been
given. Faith is the inner assurance that what we desire already exists in the invisible realm of Spirit and
can, by the *exercise* of our faith, be brought into
being.

God is the mind-stuff and substance that underlies
all manifestation. When these are acted upon by our
faith, things or outer conditions are formed. If they
are not to our liking, it is because our faith is limited,
or because it is fixed upon false gods or materialistic
goals. When faith is centered upon Him, only good
can be objectified. Everything in the formed world
has its origin in God. Understanding faith opens the
door to the faculty of intuition, which reveals this.

Many were the exploits of the great heroes of faith
in Hebrew allegory and history. By faith Abel "offered to God a more acceptable sacrifice than Cain"
(Heb. 11:4). "By faith Enoch was taken up so that
he should not see death" (Heb. 11:5). "By faith
Noah, being warned by God concerning events as yet
unseen . . . constructed an ark for the saving of his
household . . . and became an heir of the righteousness which comes by faith" (Heb. 11:7).

A lengthy section discusses Abraham who, by faith, ventured into a new land and looked for a "city which has foundations, whose builder and maker is God" (Heb. 11:10). By faith Sarah bore a son in her old age, by faith Jacob and Joseph carried on the spiritual birthright.

Moses who fled from Egypt "endured as seeing him who is invisible" (Heb. 11:27). By faith, in the days of Joshua, "the walls of Jericho fell down" (Heb. 11:30). By Rahab's faith in the justice of the Hebrews' cause her life was spared.

In closing the chapter, the author enumerates many daring men of faith from Gideon to David and the prophets,

> who through faith conquered kingdoms, enforced justice, received promises, stopped the mouths of lions, quenched raging fire, escaped the edge of the sword, won strength out of weakness, became mighty in war, put foreign armies to flight (Heb 11:33, 34).

These stories of the great accomplishments that grew from faith are most inspiring. We cannot read them without feeling an upsurge of our own faith. This is of the utmost importance for without faith, "it is impossible to please him. For whoever would draw near to God must believe that he exists and that he rewards those who seek him" (Heb. 11:6). Jesus presents the same idea in a shorter and more positive way by declaring, "All things are possible to him who believes" (Mark 9:23).

Though these mighty men of valor gained much through their faith both for themselves and their fellow men, they "did not receive what was promised" (Heb. 11:39). Complete fulfillment comes only through faith in Jesus Christ. Nevertheless their exploits serve to give us the courage to press forward, and Chapter XII begins with the charge:

> Therefore, since we are surrounded by so great a cloud of witnesses, let us also lay aside every weight, and sin which clings so closely, and let us run with perseverance the race that is set before us, looking to Jesus the pioneer and perfecter of our faith (Heb. 12:1, 2).

In referring to the suffering of Jesus, the writer discusses the suffering caused by persecution and declares that "the Lord disciplines him whom he loves and chastises every son whom he receives" (Heb. 12:6). His argument is that as a father reproves and disciplines his son, so the heavenly Father, regarding the followers of Jesus as His sons, uses discipline as a means of purifying and drawing them closer to Him. At the time such suffering seems painful, yet "later it yields the peaceful fruit of righteousness to those who have been trained by it" (Heb. 12:11).

In truth, we reject the thought that God inflicts pain upon anyone even for the sake of bringing that one to Him. We believe that all suffering is self-induced. Much of it is the result of our violation of the divine law, either intentional or through ignorance. We understand, however, that suffering can have a constructive origin, arising from our earnest desire to follow Jesus Christ. This demands spiritual development. If we aspire to be like Him, we must be able to meet each problem in a spiritual manner. All conditions that cause pain provide the opportunity to lean more trustingly upon the Lord. The problem itself is neither a punishment nor a chastisement but rather a chance to know more fully the power of God to heal and harmonize. The Christians to whom this epistle was addressed could either resist persecution to the point of forsaking their religious convictions, or rely on God to defend and deliver them.

Any situation that hurts us is actually a blessing in disguise. It gives us the privilege of saying, "When they cast *thee* down, thou shalt say, *There is* lifting up" (Job 22:29 A.S.V.). In rising above the belief that we are being chastened or disciplined by God, we move out of suffering and are lifted to the freedom that comes from knowing that He is in control and all is well.

The writer urges us to be strong so that our steadfastness will furnish strength to weaker ones. We are to keep the Christ ideal of peace and consecration in mind so as not to miss receiving the grace of God. We are not under the old covenant that was given to Moses from a mountain shrouded in mist and darkness, "but you have come to Mount Zion and to the city of the living God, the heavenly Jerusalem, and to innumerable angels" (Heb. 12:22). Listen to the divine voice! Serve God faithfully for He is a "consuming fire," and in this fire all that is unworthy shall perish.

Chapter XIII contains sundry instructions as to our right attitude toward the leaders of the church. The latter speak the word of God and we should imitate their faith. But even though these come and go, "Jesus Christ is the same yesterday and today and for ever" (Heb. 13:8).

The writer then injects the first personal note in the epistle by asking that the Christians pray for him. His prayer for them is the beautiful doxology of Hebrews 13:20,21.

James

Three men by the name of James are prominent in the New Testament. Two were among the original Twelve Apostles: James, the son of Zebedee and brother of John, and James, the son of Alphaeus, sometimes called James the Less. The third James was the head of the Christian church in Jerusalem. No mention is made of him in the Four Gospels, but he comes into the Bible narrative in The Acts. It is thought that this James was the brother or half brother of Jesus, and the brother of Jude, the writer of the epistle that bears his name. James was not a follower of Jesus during His lifetime but was converted after the resurrection. According to Paul, Jesus appeared to James (I Cor. 15:7). At the Jerusalem Conference, over which James presided, he upheld Paul's plea that Gentiles be permitted to become Christians free from the requirements of Judaism. He was a pious man and rightly called James, the Just. One tradition says he met death at the hands of the Pharisees who flung him from the tower when he refused to deny Jesus Christ; another, that the Sadducees had him stoned to death.

The epistle is addressed to Jewish Christians of the Dispersion and was probably written no earlier than A.D. 80. It is obvious that James understood Paul's teaching regarding faith. James' style of writing is similar to that of the wisdom literature of the Old Testament. He is not concerned with theological points or Christian doctrine. To him what is of the utmost importance is to unify religion with proper, spiritual behavior. How to put the Christ teaching into practice is what we all need to know more about. James tells us in quite positive terms. The gist of his message is, "Be doers of the word, and not hearers only, deceiving yourselves" (James 1:22).

James discusses various subjects as they occur to him and makes no attempt to connect his material sequentially. He gives five main points pertaining to Christian living and adds three more, briefly, in the last chapter of the epistle.

Temptation or trial is the first point he takes up. This is not to be met with resignation but with joy:

> Count it all joy, my brethren, when you meet various trials, for you know that the testing of your faith produces steadfastness. And let steadfastness have its full effect, that you may be perfect and complete, lacking in nothing (James 1:2-4).

We receive God's blessing when we meet and overcome temptation:

> Blessed is the man who endures trial, for when he has stood the test he will receive the crown of life which God has promised to those who love him (James 1:12).

We must not excuse ourself by saying that God tempts us. Temptations arise from succumbing to our own unworthy desires:

> Let no one say when he is tempted, "I am tempted by God"; for God cannot be tempted with evil and he himself tempts no one; but each person is tempted when he is lured and enticed by his own desire (James 1:13,14).

The second point James takes up is wealth, and it is one that he preaches on throughout the letter. He feels very strongly about the uncertainty of riches and the evil to which they are often put. The poor man should exult in the spiritual dignity his religion has brought him. On the other hand, the rich man, who may have lost some prestige by being a church member, should rejoice in his humiliation for this serves to remind him of the transient nature of wealth and to save him from the love of material things (James 1:9-11).

No discrimination should be made between members of the congregation. Failure to treat all members alike cannot be compensated for by righteous conduct in other areas of living, for only as we show mercy to others can God's mercy be shown us (James 2:1-13).

Wealthy persons who oppress the poor are denounced. Wealth in itself is not evil but the power it gives is often used in sinful ways. When suffering is inflicted on the poor, the rich are but laying up suffering for themselves, and James cries, "Come now, you rich, weep and howl for the miseries that are coming upon you" (James 5:1).

The third point deals with hearing and doing the word of God. There is a right way to hear and a right way to practice. We should be swift to hear but slow to speak (James 1:19-26). Cleanse your heart from impurity and malice and having heard the word, be faithful to it in daily living:

> Religion that is pure and undefiled before God and the Father is this: to visit orphans and widows in their affliction, and to keep oneself unstained from the world (James 1:27).

The writer's next or fourth point is faith and works. He contends that faith is not worthy of the name unless expressed in good works. Judaism laid great stress on the attainment of righteousness by a strict obedience to the works of the law, that is, following all the requirements thereof. To combat this, Paul taught that we can attain righteousness, or union with God, only through faith, and justification by faith in Jesus Christ forms a large part of his message. Thus many Christians jumped to the conclusion that faith alone was sufficient. Paul never meant to imply this and his letters are filled with instructions for spiritual living, morality, brotherly

love and so on. There is no real conflict between the
teaching of Paul and that of James. The latter, however, is even more emphatic in driving home his conviction that real faith and good deeds are inseparable:

> What does it profit, my brethren, if a man says he has
> faith but has no works? Can his faith save him? If a
> brother or sister is ill-clad and in lack of daily food, and
> one of you says to them, "Go in peace, be warmed and
> filled," without giving them the things needed for the
> body, what does it profit? So faith by itself, if it has no
> works, is dead.
> But some one will say, "You have faith and I have
> works." Show me your faith apart from your works,
> and I by my works will show you my faith (James
> 2:14-18).

The fifth point is wisdom and this too is discussed
intermittently through several chapters:

> If any of you lacks wisdom, let him ask God who
> gives to all men generously and without reproaching,
> and it will be given him. But let him ask in faith, with no
> doubting, for he who doubts is like a wave of the sea
> that is driven and tossed by the wind. For that person
> must not suppose that a double-minded man, unstable
> in all his ways, will receive anything from the Lord
> (James 1:5-8).

Continuing the subject of wisdom, James warns
those who are ambitious to become teachers that
they will be judged with greater severity than others.
Sins of speech are only too easily committed for
"the tongue is a fire. The tongue is an unrighteous

world among our members, staining the whole body" (James 3:6). Man can tame wild beasts, "but no human being can tame the tongue—a restless evil, full of deadly poison" (James 3:8). With the tongue we bless the Lord and, at the same time, we curse man who is made in His likeness. My brethren, this ought not to be so" (James 3:10). True wisdom is shown by meekness and the absence of jealousy and faction:

> But the wisdom from above is first pure, then peaceable, gentle, open to reason, full of mercy and good fruits, without uncertainty or insincerity (James 3:17).

James pleads for a life lived in harmony with God's will. Strife is due to lust, covetousness, and warring against one another. God cannot answer our prayers when we are in such a state of mind. "You ask and do not receive, because you ask wrongly, to spend it on your passions" (James 4:3). He counsels:

> Draw near to God and he will draw near to you. . . .
> Humble yourselves before the Lord and he will exalt you (James 4:8-10).

Be charitable in judging others and so fulfill the law of love. God should also be included in any business plans (James 4:13-17).

In the final or fifth chapter of his letter, James gives three additional essentials for Christian living: (1) patience. "You also be patient. Establish your hearts, for the coming of the Lord is at hand" (James

5:8); (2) faithfulness in prayer. When in trouble, pray; and when cheerful, sing praises unto God. Pray for the sick. This is effective indeed for "the prayer of faith will save the sick man, and the Lord will raise him up; and if he have committed sins, he will be forgiven" (James 5:15); (3) turning others from their misdeeds. "Let him know that whoever brings back a sinner from the error of his way will save his soul from death and will cover a multitude of sins" (James 5:20).

General Epistles (II)

I Peter; I, II, III John;
Jude; II Peter

There is much uncertainty among Bible scholars regarding the authorship and date of these six letters. They were written to handle urgent matters confronting the churches. Scattered over a large area, these were exposed to diverse teachings and needed the counsel and encouragement of the ones who had known Jesus Christ or been closely associated with those who had. Whenever there is a demand there is always an adequate supply, and as the followers of the Master made their demand the supply of enlightenment and strength flowed to them from these stalwart apostles and their followers.

The two main problems of the moment were: first, persecution which bid fair to decimate the church, and second, the false teachings of Gnosticism and Antinomianism (immorality) which threatened to undermine the gospel of Jesus Christ. All these letters, with the exception of III John which is of a personal nature, discuss these subjects.

I Peter

This is known as a "persecution letter." It is difficult for us to envision a time when being a follower of Jesus Christ could present grave danger, subjecting a person to oppression and often a cruel death.

As Tertullian, one of the early church fathers, said, "The blood of martyrs is the seed of the Church," and indeed it was by the stanch faith and unflagging courage of these martyrs that the church was able to survive. Not until the Emperor Constantine gave his approval to Christianity, in A.D. 313, did the persecutions cease entirely.

In the day of the writing of I Peter, every Christian had to decide whether he was willing to undergo hardship or death for his loyalty to Christ, or whether he would deny Him and save himself. The writer was well aware of the dilemma, and he tells the believer not to rebel against persecution but to rely completely upon Christ, and to rejoice that he is considered worthy to follow in His footsteps.

Though we are not subjected today to physical danger because of our religious beliefs, we do experience periods that are similar to the times of ill-treatment accorded the early Christians. These take the form of injustice, criticism, slander, and actual abuse inflicted upon us by others. We need to know the most effective way of dealing with these. Our attitude toward them has much to do with the effect they have upon us. I Peter is one of the finest expressions in the Bible or elsewhere on how to meet tribulations in a spiritual way.

The letter was addressed to Christians in Asia Minor, threatened with persecution by the Roman government. The general consensus is that the letter was written during the time of either the Neronian or the Domitian persecutions in Rome (if by Peter himself, probably shortly before his own martyrdom, about A.D. 64, otherwise about A.D. 96).

A spirit of hope and triumph pervades the epistle. We are exhorted to give thanks to God for the "inheritance which is imperishable" (I Pet. 1:4) that we have received from Jesus Christ, and for the glory that shall be ours. The trials of the present are only temporary. They prove our faith and serve to purify us as fire purifies gold. Though we have not seen Jesus, our love for Him and confidence in His saving grace fill our heart with joy. Great teachers (prophets) foretold a period of suffering which would be followed by the triumph of the Spirit of Christ:

> Therefore gird up your minds, be sober, set your hope fully upon the grace that is coming to you at the revelation of Jesus Christ (I Peter 1:13).

Such a hope should make for holy living, for we are redeemed "not with perishable things ... but with the precious blood of Christ" (I Pet. 1:18, 19). As He was victorious over death so, with Him, we shall rise above our trials. We are no longer bound to the flesh but are living a higher type of life.

We are to put away all evildoing, for we are richly blessed. As a newborn babe, "long for the pure spiritual milk, that by it you may grow up to salvation" (I Pet. 2:2). We are stones in a living temple of which Jesus Christ is the chief cornerstone (I Pet. 2:3-7). Also,

> you are a chosen race, a royal priesthood, a holy

nation, God's own people, that you may declare the
wonderful deeds of him who called you out of darkness
into his marvelous light (I Peter 2:9).

We should conduct ourself like a follower of the
Lord and honor Him in all that we do. If persecuted,
we should endure with faith in Him. Unbelievers
who would speak evil against us will see our good
works and glorify God (I Pet. 2:11-25).

Let wives and husbands live at peace with one
another. Be charitable toward all in a spirit of loving
fellowship (I Pet. 3:7-12). No one can harm us when
we are zealous for what is good. Even if we are called
upon to suffer for the sake of righteousness, we
should not fear:

> but in your hearts reverence Christ as Lord. Always
> be prepared to make a defense to any one who calls you
> to account for the hope that is in you, yet do it with
> gentleness and reverence; and keep your conscience
> clear, so that, when you are abused, those who revile
> your good behavior in Christ may be put to shame. For
> it is better to suffer for doing right, if that should be
> God's will, than for doing wrong (I Peter 3:15-17).

Jesus suffered that He might bring us to God, so
"arm yourselves with the same thought" (I Pet. 4:1).
Some may think it strange that we do not enter into
their way of life, and speak critically of us. We
should ignore this and live the Christ life as we were
taught: "Above all hold unfailing your love for one
another, since love covers a multitude of sins" (I Pet.
4:8).

Faith in undergoing trials proves our worth. We should rejoice in afflictions. We are not being punished as a criminal, "yet if one suffers as a Christian, let him not be ashamed, but under that name let him glorify God" (I Pet. 4:16).

Leaders or elders in the church should willingly "tend the flock of God," and make themselves examples. When the chief Shepherd comes He will give them a crown of glory:

> Humble yourselves therefore under the mighty hand of God, that in due time he may exalt you. Cast all your anxieties on him, for he cares about you. Be sober, be watchful. Your adversary the devil prowls around like a roaring lion, seeking some one to devour (I Peter 5:6-8).

> Be steadfast, and God "will himself restore, establish, and strengthen you" (I Pet. 5:10).

The Gospel of John, the three epistles of John, and Revelation are known as the Johannine books of the New Testament. Whether only the Gospel or all of these were written by the apostle John is a question that has not been answered satisfactorily despite endless research.

I and II John combat Gnosticism. This had already made its appearance in the church in the time of Paul, who took vigorous exception to the heresy in his letter to the Colossians. When John wrote more than a quarter of a century later, Gnosticism was having a more profound effect on the church's teaching. What these Christian leaders considered heretical was the Gnostic claim that its adherents possessed superior knowledge which absolved them from sin; also Docetism, a form of Gnosticism, which held the Incarnation to be in appearance only (which meant that the human life of Jesus was unreal). John sternly denied that such teachings had any place in Christianity.

First-century followers of Christ had many problems in connection with their religious beliefs. Today we can turn to the New Testament for confirmation of our faith, but the early Christians had no such support. Though the Four Gospels had been written and the letters of Paul were widely circulated, none of these had the authority then that the ages have given them. Neither did the church have a creed or statement of faith, such as was developed later. It was left to the wisdom and discretion of the few who had been with Jesus, or had been taught by an apostle, to decide what should or should not be accepted by the church.

The principle underlying Gnosticism is with us today in those who consider that their particular belief is superior to any other, either in other religions or in another denomination of the Christian faith. All ways that lead to the Supreme Being have merit, and no one way is wholly right to the exclusion of all others. A holier-than-thou attitude is unacceptable in the true follower of Jesus Christ. As we "will to do His will" we are drawn to whatever teaching is most helpful to us just where we are in our own development.

As Truth students, we are plagued by the false teaching of our erroneous belief in the reality of evil or limitation. Our fundamental tenet of faith is "God, the good, is all there is." We accept Him as the one reality, and this is consistent with our interpretation of the Bible. Yet we continue to acknowledge the absence of God when limitation makes its appearance. Lack of good *seems* so real that it is often well-nigh impossible to refute its claim. The person that we actually are, a child of our heavenly Father with access to all the qualities and powers of the indwelling Christ, vies with the appearance that we are a mortal being and victim of the various ills of mortality.

The erroneous thoughts and feelings that tell us we are bound by this or that lack and entice us to yield to discouragement, resentment, and sorrow establish adverse states of consciousness against which Jesus warned us by saying, "A man's foes will be those of his own household" (Matt. 10:36). It is difficult to believe that our only enemies are within ourself. The first step is to deny their spurious claims, and then affirm the Truth. Only steadfast faith can guard us against the onslaughts of those mental and emotional foes that tempt us to accept anything less than the whole Truth—the allness of God in which we live, move, and have our being. These stern letters denouncing false teachings with intensity also point out the necessity for complete loyalty to our Lord's words.

In his first epistle, John speaks often of our short-comings, or sins as he calls them, and insists that we recognize and repent of them. The emphasis of the letter, however, is on love, the love of God for us, and our love for Him and for our fellow man. These are the sections we remember best and which inspire in us a desire to be worthy of His love. Throughout this epistle John echoes Paul's conviction that love never fails, and that it alone is the fulfilling of the law.

I John

It is generally conceded that the apostle John wrote this from Ephesus in the last decade of the first Christian century. It is not addressed to any church and is more of a treatise than a letter.

The epistle begins on a high spiritual note, as does the Gospel of John. God is light. The writer uses the word *light* as a symbol of perfect righteousness. To have fellowship with Him we must walk in the light and accept the cleansing offered through Jesus Christ (I John 1:7). No one should claim that he is without sin because of his professed knowledge:

> If we say we have no sin, we deceive ourselves, and the truth is not in us. If we confess our sins, he is faithful and just, and will forgive our sins and cleanse us from all unrighteousness (I John 1:8, 9).

We are urged to walk in the true light of love:

> He who says he is in the light and hates his brother is
> in the darkness still. He who loves his brother abides in
> the light, and in it there is no cause for stumbling (I
> John 2:9,10).

John tells us not to set our affection on material things for "the world passes away, and the lust of it; but he who does the will of God abides for ever" (I John 2:17). We are to beware of the antichrist, a symbol of evil, to which false teachers are compared. They are ignorant but "you have been anointed by the Holy One, and you all know" (I John 2:20). They deny the Father and the Son, but we have confessed the Son and therefore have the Father also. We are to abide in Him.

Chapter three begins with the familiar and beautiful words describing the Father's love for us:

> See what love the Father has given us, that we should
> be called children of God; and so we are. The reason
> why the world does not know us is that it did not know
> him. Beloved, we are God's children now; it does not
> yet appear what we shall be, but we know that when he
> appears we shall be like him, for we shall see him as he is
> (I John 3:1, 2).

With this glorious hope in our heart we should wish to prepare ourself to accept His love fully. This requires more than the superficial purifications practiced by those who give scant attention to their transgressions. The Son of God came that He might destroy sin, the work of the devil. Whoever is begotten of God is so transformed that he cannot sin (I John 3:3-12).

Our love should be concretely demonstrated: "Little children, let us not love in word or speech but in deed and in truth" (I John 3:18). Love frees us from a feeling of unworthiness and instills in us a joyful trust in Him to respond to our every call (I John 3:19-24).

In the fifteen verses, I John 4:7-21, John uses the word *love* some twenty-five times. This passage is a noteworthy rival to I Corinthians 13. "God is love," and He proved His love for us by sending His Son into the world that we might live through Him. We are able to love because God first loved us: "And this commandment we have from him, that he who loves God should love his brother also" (I John 4:21).

If we believe that Jesus Christ is begotten of God, we love both the Father and the Son and keep the divine commandments. They are not grievous: "For whatever is born of God overcomes the world; and this is the victory that overcomes the world, our faith. Who is it that overcomes the world but he who believes that Jesus is the Son of God?" (I John 5:4).

Chapter five again refers to sin, declaring, "There is sin which is mortal" (I John 5:16), that is, an unpardonable sin. Jesus had stated, "Every sin and blasphemy will be forgiven men, but the blasphemy against the Spirit will not be forgiven" (Matt. 12:31). In Truth, we believe that as long as we deny the Holy Spirit by living apart from God, our existence becomes increasingly unfruitful. In time, however, each soul, weary of suffering, turns to the Father and is forgiven. John seems to retreat from his rigid position by saying, "All wrongdoing is sin, but there is sin which is not mortal" (I John 5:17).

In the last section of the letter, I John 5:18-21, the writer refutes the claim of those who consider that theirs is the true knowledge by saying that Christians possess a trinity of knowledge: (1) We know that the child of God does not sin; (2) We know that we are of God though the world is still under control of the "evil one"; (3) We know that the Son of God has come to the world and has given us the understanding that our real life is in Jesus Christ.

II John

This is the shortest book in the Bible, consisting of one chapter of thirteen verses. The author refers to himself as the "elder," which makes it uncertain as to whether or not it was written by John the Apostle, but because of the similarity in subject matter and expression, it seems probable that it was written by the author of I John.

The letter is addressed to the "elect lady and her children," meaning a specific church and its members. In content it is a sharp warning against false teachers. In those days there were itinerant preachers who went from one church to another, and many of them were sincere Christian missionaries. Some, however, took advantage of this custom to teach things that were contrary to the Gospel and thereby caused much confusion. The writer insists that those "who will not acknowledge the coming of Jesus Christ in the flesh" (II John 1:7) are not to be tolerated and should be sent on their way without even bidding them Godspeed!

John explains that he is writing briefly, as he hopes to come and see them soon and talk face to face.

III John

This is another short letter, and again the author refers to himself as the "elder." It is addressed to Gaius, who was evidently the leader of a church in the vicinity of Ephesus and not the Gaius who was the convert and friend of Paul. The letter is confidential and deals with a troublesome situation in the church. It does not touch on any religious questions and is interesting to us only as revealing that even when the church was making a courageous effort to survive, it had to contend with those who were striving for power.

After a warm greeting to Gaius, John complains of one Diotrephes whom he describes as a man "who likes to put himself first" (III John 1:9). Diotrephes exerted much influence in the church and was refusing to receive and entertain worthy visiting missionaries as well as causing other members to do likewise or be excommunicated.

To Gaius, John says:

Beloved, do not imitate evil but imitate good. He

who does good is of God; he who does evil has not seen
God (III John 11).

The writer commends another member, Demetrius, of whom all speak well. He says he will soon visit
the church and discuss these matters.

Jude

The epistle was meant for general circulation, as it
was not addressed to any church. The writer calls
himself Jude, the brother of James, which would
make him one of the brethren of Jesus Christ. It is
the opinion among scholars, however, that the letter
deals with a situation that did not develop in the
church until the last part of the first century.

The writer attacks that phase of the false teaching
known as Antinomianism, or the belief that the
moral law is unnecessary. There had been flagrant
immorality in the church in the days of Paul (though
it was apparently restricted to individual members),
but now there were those in the position of teachers
who condoned and even advocated immoral practices. These Jude denounces with violence.

The church of today continues to wrestle with
this type of false teaching. Immorality is still to be
seen in the dishonesty, injustice, and greed that far
too often blacken the character of Christ's followers.
Virtue among Christians, as well as among non-Chris-
tians, is at a premium. Jesus' command, "Do not
resist one who is evil," is not an invitation to suc-

cumb to evil, and we are called upon to resist the
insidious temptation to follow the desires of the
flesh. There is a great need to renew our love for the
beauty of holiness.

A still higher degree of morality is incumbent
upon the Truth student who understands that the
thought, with feeling, is father of the act. We are
challenged to cleanse our consciousness, and this can
be accomplished only by substituting the spiritual
for the carnal thought.

At the start of his letter Jude says that he wants to
write his fellow Christians in a spiritual vein and discuss their common salvation. But, instead, he feels
impelled to urge them to support the faith against
those ungodly persons who have come into the
church "who pervert the grace of our God into licentiousness and deny our only Master and Lord, Jesus
Christ" (Jude 1:4).

Divine punishment will surely overtake sinners
such as the false teachers who are leading others
astray. The writer cites a number of examples from
Jewish history of those who had fallen from grace,
beginning with the Children of Israel who failed to
reach the Promised Land. The inhabitants of Sodom
and Gomorrah, who indulged in various forms of
immorality, were destroyed. And "in like manner
these men in their dreamings defile the flesh, reject
authority, and revile the glorious ones" (Jude 1:8).
Such look down upon the instruction of true Christian teachers and resist all authority. They are bringing ultimate destruction upon themselves, as did

Cain, Balaam, and Korah.

At the love feasts (common meals) these teachers are a menace, for they feed themselves rather than the needy. Jude gives a graphic description of their deceptive ways:

> These are blemishes on your love feasts, as they boldly carouse together, looking after themselves; waterless clouds, carried along by winds; fruitless trees in late autumn, twice dead, uprooted, wild waves of the sea, casting up the foam of their own shame; wandering stars for whom the nether gloom of darkness has been reserved for ever (Jude 12, 13).

We are not to be astonished at the presence of such people in the church, for it has been prophesied in the Book of Enoch (an Apocryphal work) that God would send an angelic host to execute judgment. These false teachers murmur and complain, yet they continue to follow their own lustful desires and are not above paying respect to those they think can advance them:

> But you, beloved, build yourselves up on your most holy faith; pray to the Holy Spirit; keep yourselves in the love of God; wait for the mercy of our Lord Jesus Christ unto eternal life (Jude 20, 21).

We should show kindness to offenders in our midst who may be saved from their evil ways. Others who have drifted further from the right course will require more strenuous efforts to reform. But we should protect ourself against those who have completely forsaken the Christian ideal and guard against any undue contact with them (Jude 22, 23).

The letter ends with a benediction committing the faithful to their God through Jesus Christ, our Lord.

II Peter

The writer calls himself Simon Peter, the apostle of Jesus Christ, and parts of the letter may well have been written by him. But if so, considerable additions were made by an unknown writer, probably a disciple of Peter, at a much later time. The date of writing is generally given as the middle of the second century, which makes this letter the last-written book of the New Testament. The subject matter is similar to that of Jude's epistle, and one commentator refers to it as "Jude enlarged to three chapters." II Peter was evidently intended for the church in general, as it was not addressed to any one church.

The letter is an attack on false teachers who are advocating and practicing immorality.

Peter says that the promises of God have been made available to us by Jesus Christ, and through them we may become partakers of the divine nature and escape the corruption that is in the world (II Pet. 1:4):

> For this very reason make every effort to supplement your faith with virtue, and virtue with knowledge, and knowledge with self-control, and self-control with steadfastness, and steadfastness with godliness,

and godliness with brotherly affection, and brotherly affection with love (II Pet. 1:5-7).

If we fail to develop these virtues, we are short-sighted and may even wonder why we were cleansed of our former deficiencies. Peter says that we really know these things, but that he is reminding us of them again.

Christianity rests upon a firm foundation of fact, attested to by eyewitnesses to the glory of Jesus Christ. Moreover, believers have the truths contained in the Old Testament, which prophesies events to transpire in the future (II Pet. 1:12-21). But prophecy is subject to interpretation and there have been false prophets, even as there are now false teachers who give forth destructive heresies, "denying the Master who bought them, bringing upon themselves swift destruction" (II Pet. 2:1).

The divine judgment is to be doled out mainly to those "who indulge in the lust of defiling passion" (II Pet. 2:10). They resist all authority. "These are waterless springs and mists driven by a storm; for them the nether gloom of darkness has been reserved" (II Pet. 2:17). They entice those who are not fully grounded in faith, promising liberty though they themselves are bound to utter depravity:

> For if, after they have escaped the defilements of the world through the knowledge of our Lord and Savior Jesus Christ, they are again entangled in them and overpowered, the last state has become worse for them than the first. For it would have been better for them never

to have known the way of righteousness than after knowing it to turn back from the holy commandment delivered to them (II Peter 2:20, 21).

Peter lays great stress on the "day of the Lord." The idea of the destruction of the world and a final judgment was a Jewish concept. It had been borrowed by the first-century Christians and connected with the Second Coming of Christ. It was believed that "the day of the Lord" was imminent. As time passed and the momentous event did not take place, some discarded the teaching and grew so lax in conduct that the leaders of the church feared an increasing moral breakdown. Peter tries to halt this by assuring the faithful that judgment for sinners would surely come:

> The day of the Lord will come like a thief, and then the heavens will pass away with a loud noise, and the elements will be dissolved with fire, and the earth and the works that are upon it will be burned up (II Peter 3:10).

He pleads with Christians to live a blameless life so that they may be found worthy to enter the "new heavens and a new earth" which will be established at His coming.

Isolated references to the destruction of the world, which occur in several places in the Bible, have caused some Christian denominations to fear God's judgment. As Truth students, we understand that it is not fear that induces righteousness. Only love for Him and a desire to emulate Jesus Christ can inspire us to want to obey His whole law. We do not believe that Jesus' prediction of the end of the world means the destruction of the earth. Modern translators render this clause the "close of the age," and Charles Fillmore says:

> Jesus Christ never taught that God would destroy the earth, but He did teach that race evolution was being carried forward in great periods or ages, one of which was ending in His time. Jesus said that no one knew the duration of this age except the Father (KL 27).

Applied individually, the "close of the age" is the termination of a period of our life. We pass through many ages or worlds in one existence. The law of cause and effect is ever operative and is not confined to a final judgment at death, nor to the actual Second Coming of Christ in the flesh. Surely we agree with the plea Peter makes for right conduct, for we know that a high moral standard is the only thing consistent with faith in Jesus Christ. The pure in heart see God, and when we are pure in our feeling nature (heart) that purity extends to our outer life as well.

Peter ends his letter with the admonition to "grow in the grace and knowledge of our Lord and Savior Jesus Christ" (II Pet. 3:18).

The New Birth
Revelation 1–3

It is indeed fitting that the New Testament, which begins with the angel annunciation of the coming of Christ, should conclude with a vision of "a new heaven and a new earth" manifest for the one who expresses the Christ. Of Revelation Charles Fillmore says, "Jesus, the Great Teacher, gave many lessons for our instruction, the greatest and most mystical being the Revelation of John" (TM 7). Because Revelation deals wholly with states of consciousness and does not mean what it says in a literal sense, it is undoubtedly the least understood book in the Bible. A literal interpretation leads to the utmost confusion. John, the Revelator, deliberately disguised his meaning by using symbols, and neither in the first nor the twentieth century could his book be understood without a conscientious effort to discover the spiritual significance of his remarkable visions.

"The Revelation to John," or simply "Revelation" as the book is commonly called, belongs to a type of writing known as apocalyptic. The word is derived from the Greek meaning "uncovered, unveiled, revealed." Its purpose is to reveal hidden truths. This particular type of writing developed greatly among the Jews in the second century B. C. and extended into the Christian era. Daniel is the chief apocalypse of the Old Testament, though parts of Isaiah, Joel, and Zechariah also belong to this group, and were inserted into the original books at a later date.

The Jewish apocalypses were written to give consolation to their people during periods of despair and persecution. The writers offer hope and encouragement to the distressed by reminding them of God's love and power as shown in the past, and promise even greater expressions of them in the future. The trying and dangerous times made it necessary for the authors to use symbols so that if their documents fell into the hands of enemies they would be meaningless. The symbols were understood by the people for whom the apocalypses were written. For example, the Jews suffering persecution at the hands of the Syrians in the second century B. C. knew that the term "abomination of desolation," used in Daniel, referred to the desecration of the temple by Antiochus Epiphanes.

Revelation is the only apocalypse in the New Testament. Its obvious purpose was to fortify Christians who were being persecuted by the Roman government. Paul had established Christian groups throughout the Mediterranean area and for a decade these grew and flourished, undisturbed by the Romans. The first persecution took place in Rome under Nero about A.D. 64, but it was not until the reign of the Emperor Domitian (A.D. 81-96) that it became widespread. The Roman emperors called themselves gods and demanded worship in the pagan temples throughout the empire. This was the spark that fired the conflict between the Roman authorities and the followers of Jesus Christ. Though some Christians complied, the majority did not. As punishment some were banished, some imprisoned, and many slain. John sought to give comfort to these stanch defenders of the faith and promised deliverance to those who remained true to their Savior.

Revelation was included in the New Testament canon because, for generations, it was thought to have been written by John, the Apostle of Jesus Christ. There is a diversity of opinion among scholars as to whether the apostle John or another man of that name wrote the book. It seems certain that it was written before the Gospel of John but after the fall of Jerusalem in A.D. 70. The most likely date is the last decade of the first century.

According to early tradition, the apostle John became the head of the Christian church in Ephesus and during the persecution was exiled to Patmos, a small island in the Aegean Sea off the coast of Asia Minor. The Romans had large quarries there and the place was used as a penal colony. While on Patmos, John transcribed the visions that comprise Revelation. However, most contemporary scholars attribute the book to John, the Elder.

The writer used symbols for the same reason that the Jews did, that is, to disguise his meaning. The Christians of his day would understand what he intended to convey. It was clear to them that "Babylon" referred to Rome. Babylon had been the wicked city of ancient days as Rome was of the present. They had no trouble in discerning that the Lamb and the Child born of the woman represented Jesus Christ. They also understood why John wrote such frightening visions in the body of the book. There was a belief among Christians, borrowed from the Jews, that God would intervene in human affairs and deliver the faithful. When He did, a new age of justice and peace would ensue. It was believed, however, that evil must reach a climax before God would take charge of things. The tumult to precede His coming was termed the "Messianic Woes," and these John pictures vividly. Most of the symbols used in Revelation were taken from various Old Testament books, especially Ezekiel.

Revelation may be divided into four parts:

1. Prologue: Vision of Christ, Letters to Churches (Rev. 1–3).

2. Six Visions of Trial, and Final Victory (Rev. 4–20).
    a. Throne of God, and the Lamb (Rev. 4, 5).
    b. Opening of Seven-Sealed Book (Rev. 6, 7).
    c. Sounding of Seven Trumpets (Rev. 8–11).
    d. The Woman, Child, and Dragon (Rev. 12–14).
    e. Pouring of Seven Bowls (Rev. 15–18).
    f. Victory of Christ (Rev. 19, 20).

3. Seventh Vision, New Heaven and New Earth (Rev. 21-22:5).

4. Epilogue: Seven Admonitions, Benediction (Rev. 22:6-21).

As Truth students we do not limit the interpretation of Revelation to a prediction of historical events to transpire in the immediate or distant future. We believe John had a twofold purpose. First, he wanted to assure Christians of his day that God is all-powerful to save those who trust Him. For all generations of Christians the obvious lesson to be drawn is that, regardless of the almost overwhelming power of evil, spiritual forces are even stronger. Despite the seemingly revengeful tone in parts of the book, which is so unlike the teaching of love given by Jesus Christ, Revelation has earned its place in Scripture because of its insistence that God is in control of the world and its supreme confidence that divine justice and peace will eventually prevail.

John's second and most important purpose in writing Revelation was to furnish a chart to the spiritual aspirant in his quest for union with the indwelling Christ. Charles Fillmore states: "The key to every problem in the universe is the figure one. . . . The only way to get at the inner truth of any scripture is to start with the assumption that it treats of *man* as an individual" (Unity, Vol. 36, pg. 208). He further states that Revelation is "a picture of redeemed man and the process of his redemption."

In conversing with Nicodemus, Jesus said, "Unless one is born anew, he cannot see the kingdom of God" (John 3:3). Revelation is the story of the birth of the initiate into spiritual consciousness and the heights to which this leads him.

> Nearly all of the Book of Revelation is taken up with
> a mystical history of the experiences in the minds and
> bodies of those who go into this temple within and
> make the mighty initiations and overcomings which
> ultimate in the visibility of the Son of God.
> *(Unity, Vol. 36, pg. 209)*

Let the one who has eyes to see and ears to hear
realize that this book gives an accurate account of his
own spiritual journey from the moment of his first
vivid awakening to the reality of spiritual man, to the
day of his full expression of that man. Jesus Christ
proved that man is a spiritual being and master of
himself and all that concerns him. Revelation confirms this and is applicable to every individual who
makes up his mind to follow the Christ. Only he can
know the pain and the joy of that rebirth which
opens the door to the kingdom of God.

At the start of our spiritual quest, two states of
consciousness are present in us, the Christ or higher
consciousness, and the mortal or lower consciousness. The former is innate for we are children of God,
but it cannot express fully until it is acknowledged
and activated by our own conscious effort: the latter
has developed because of our ignorance of God,
which has given rise to negative thinking, feeling,
speaking, and acting. When we come to ourself, as it
were, and realize that union with the indwelling
Christ is the supreme goal of the soul, we are ready
for the lessons Revelation teaches. It lays down the
way of the spiritual seeker, a way that is straight and
narrow.

Jesus warned, "In the world you have tribulation." We know full well the trials that develop from mortal consciousness, "but be of good cheer, I have overcome the world" (John 16:33). As Christ rules in us, our worldly or outer tribulations are dissolved. In symbolic language, Revelation provides definite instructions for making the transition from the bondage of the mortal to the freedom of the spiritual. It is a prophesy of the victory of spiritual man, the fulfillment of Paul's prediction, "Just as we have borne the image of the man of dust, we shall also bear the image of the man of heaven" (I Cor. 15:49).

Vision of Christ
Revelation 1

The prologue, consisting of this vision and the letters to the seven churches, begins by making it plain that this is the "revelation of Jesus Christ," given to John, His servant. The revealing of truth can come only from the One who declared, "I am the way, and the truth, and the life," and can be received only by the one who can bear "witness to the word of God and to the testimony of Jesus Christ." We, as individual seekers after God, are identified with John, who represents the love quality in consciousness. It is our love for the Lord and our intense desire to obey Him that qualifies us as spiritual aspirant or initiate.

Usually our first conscious spiritual awakening

comes at a time when we are experiencing difficulties (John was a prisoner on the isle of Patmos). As we pray ("in the Spirit on the Lord's day"), suddenly we are conscious of receiving clear and strong guidance (hear "behind me a loud voice like a trumpet"), instructing us to give forth the Word (write to the seven churches). We want to be sure from whence this guidance is coming (turn "to see the voice that was speaking"), and we know it is from God for a vision of His Son appears to us:

> I saw seven golden lampstands, and in the midst of the lampstands one like a son of man, clothed with a long robe and with a golden girdle round his breast; his head and his hair were white as white wool, white as snow; his eyes were like a flame of fire, his feet were like burnished bronze, refined as in a furnace, and his voice was like the sound of many waters; in his right hand he held seven stars, from his mouth issued a sharp two-edged sword, and his face was like the sun shining in full strength (Rev. 1:12-16).

This is our first encounter with the symbols with which Revelation abounds. They seem fantastic, and yet ordinary words are inadequate to express the splendor of a spiritual vision. We do not see an ordinary man but an extraordinary one, and only extravagant words can portray Him. The mystics of all religions have described their flashes of cosmic consciousness in like manner. The vision is meant to convey the greatness, the magnificence, the splendor of the Son of God.

The vision is also our first acquaintance with the wonderful order that underlies the construction of the book. Like the tones of a great symphony, Revelation moves in a majestic rhythm that no discord mars. It is the symphony of the soul in which the major and minor chords follow one another in orderly procession to the climax. The whole structure is based on the sacred numbers, seven and twelve. Seven is the Hebrew number signifying completeness, such as the seven days of creation. In Revelation the number is used prolifically, as seven letters, seven-sealed book, Lamb with seven horns and seven eyes, and so on. These denote completeness in its constructive aspect. But seven can also be used to indicate complete evil, such as the dragon and beast with seven heads. The number twelve is also used repeatedly, as we shall see later on. This always indicates spiritual completeness.

As to the spiritual meaning of the above vision Charles Fillmore says:

> This description of the appearance of Jesus is partly symbolical, because John did not himself understand the full import of the powers that were being exercised by the spiritual man, whose words were so clear-cut that they appeared to John as a two-edged sword; whose eyes were so discerning that they seemed a flame of fire; whose voice was like the rippling of many waters. Language is poor and bare when one seeks to describe the glories of the spiritual state. Comparisons within the comprehension of the reader are necessary, and they but tamely tell of the superhuman man and his powers.

However, this pen picture by John of what he saw when he was lifted up "in the Spirit on the Lord's day" gives us a glimpse of what the redeemed man is like, and what we shall attain when we "awake, with thy likeness." . . .

It should be thoroughly understood that this sight of Jesus that was given to John was not a vision of a man who had died and gone to heaven up in the skies, but it was the opening of John's eyes to existence in what may be termed the fourth-dimension man (TM 7, 8).

We, the initiate, are prostrated by the vision ("I fell at his feet as though dead"), but are told not to be afraid for Christ is supreme ("I am the first and the last, and the living one"). Such a profound awareness of the reality of spiritual man is necessary as a prelude to our climb to spiritual heights. It can come in many forms. Each of us has his own unique awakening, such as came to Moses at the burning bush, and to Paul on the road to Damascus, to bring to us the realization of the nearness, the radiance, and the power of the Christ.

Our instruction is to give forth what has been revealed ("write what you see").

Letters to the Seven Churches
Revelation 2, 3

Though a perception of the Christ presence is the foundation upon which spiritual development is built, there is much to be done in the soul before Christ can be expressed through us. The churches represent states of consciousness that have become established through the long life of the soul. "The [churches] are the lights [faculties] in the individual through which he comes in touch with God within and the world without." The spiritualizing of our faculties is vital to progress. The messages, therefore, contain instructions for cleansing our mind of certain errors and strengthening certain virtues. This is necessary to prepare us for meeting the challenges that lie ahead.

The messages are constructed on a sevenfold basis: (1) Christ is the instructor as shown by the fact that each description has one or more characteristics of Christ as described in the initial vision; (2) Each message makes an appeal to the "angel of the church," that is, the divine idea in consciousness; (3) The virtues of each state of consciousness are commended; (4) The faults of each are specified and the remedy given for their cure; (5) It is pointed out how the divine law will operate unless the correction is made; (6) A blessing is promised when the faults are overcome; (7) The advice is given to listen well to these instructions.

Read Chapter 2:1-7. The divine idea in consciousness, represented by the angel of the first church, Ephesus, is addressed as Him who "holds the seven stars in his right hand, who walks among the seven golden lampstands." This is Christ as light or wisdom. Ephesus signifies "the central, building faculty of the consciousness called desire" (MD 203). It is desire that always motivates us to action on the spiritual, mental, and physical planes. Our desire can be expressed in constructive or destructive ways. When functioning in mortal consciousness our desires are focused on mental and material things. In its highest expression our desire is to know God.

Christ commends us for the progress we have made ("You are enduring patiently and bearing up for my name's sake, and you have not grown weary"). Nevertheless, there is an element in us that is gradually drifting away from singleness of purpose and purity of thought ("You have abandoned the love you had at first"). We start with a great yearning for God but, in time, our desire is likely to waver. We undergo periods of sluggishness when our enthusiasm wanes. Made in the image and likeness of God, we should not descend from that high estate ("Remember then from what you have fallen"). Spirit cautions us to do the work we did when our desire was directed toward God ("Repent and do the works you did at first"). Unless this is done the divine law will deprive us of insight or wisdom ("I will come to you and remove your lampstand from its place").

> "To him who conquers I will grant to eat of the tree of life, which is in the paradise of God" (Rev. 2:7).

To conquer is to move from mortal to spiritual thought. To gain the blessing from this promise we must rise above the inertia of the mortal self and accelerate our desire for God. Then only can we partake of the ever-renewing, vitalizing Christ ("tree of life") within ourself ("paradise of God").

Read Chapter 2:8-11. The angel of the second church, Smyrna, is addressed by "the first and the last, who died and came to life." This is Christ as quickening power, everlasting life. Smyrna symbolizes the consciousness of substance (MD 623). God is substance and underlies all manifestation. A realization of divine substance is developed as we progress spiritually.

We are praised for the fortitude with which we have borne hardships ("tribulation and . . . poverty"), but are told that we actually have plenty ("you are rich"). Often we consider ourself poor in spiritual endowment as well as worldly goods, and need to be reminded of our true wealth in both inner and outer blessings.

Our attention is called to the danger of deception by ideas that seem to be spiritual but actually belong to the mortal mind ("those who say that they are Jews and are not, but are a synagogue of Satan"). If we allow ourself to be deceived by them we will be deprived of our rightful freedom ("the devil is about to throw some of you into prison"). The statement "For ten days you will have tribulation" refers to the indefinite time required to dissolve the error thoughts. If we will keep our faith in God during this period, our reward will be a greater realization of the full life of Spirit ("Be faithful unto death, and I will give you the crown of life").

"He who conquers shall not be hurt by the second death" (Rev. 2:11).

The second death refers to the dissolution of the body. Death is the result of the destructive thoughts and emotions that are permitted to take root and grow in consciousness. When these are erased physical death cannot occur. The quickening life of Spirit renews soul and body.

Read Chapter 2:12-17. The angel of the third church, Pergamum, is addressed as "him who has the sharp two-edged sword." Christ as the power of the Word gives this message. Pergamum signifies the intellectual consciousness (MD 514). The intellect is a very important part of us, for without it we could not grasp spiritual ideas. Its true purpose is to give us an understanding of the omnipresence of God. Yet the intellect can be a deterrent to spiritual progress if it accepts false teachings, which it is very apt to do.

Our faithfulness to the Lord, even in trying times, is approved ("you hold fast my name and you did not deny my faith"), but there remains in us a strong temptation to be distracted by practices that make for idolatry, that lead to immorality, and that confuse the mind with a mixture of beliefs (teaching of Balaam, practice immorality, hold to the teaching of the Nicolaitans). Balaam was a famous character of the Old Testament who was an idol worshiper, and the Nicolaitans were a religious sect of the day whose doctrine was in opposition to Christianity.

Unless we repent and turn to God we will no longer be receptive to the word of Truth ("I will come to you soon and war against them with the sword of my mouth").

"To him who conquers I will give some of the hidden
manna, and I will give him a white stone, with a new
name written on the stone which no one knows except
him who receives it" (Rev. 2:17).

The hidden manna is our spiritual food, the Word
of God. The white stone represents the consciousness that has been purified, and the new name is I
AM. This is our spiritual name and we can claim it
only when we have learned to express our Christ
nature.

Read Chapter 2:18-29. The angel of the fourth
church, Thyatira, is addressed as "the son of God,
who has eyes like a flame of fire, and whose feet are
like burnished bronze." This is Christ as spiritual
perception and understanding. Thyatira represents
"the intense desire of the soul for the higher expressions of life [zeal]" (MD 654). Zeal is the motive
power of our being, the quality so necessary for
accomplishment.

We are zealous to serve Christ, and John recognizes this ("I know your works, your love and faith
and service and patient endurance"). On the other
hand, zeal can lead us astray when we permit it to be
attached to unworthy desires ("you tolerate the
woman Jezebel, who calls herself a prophetess and is
teaching and beguiling my servants to practice immorality"). Jezebel was the heathen queen of Israel
who was determined to force the Hebrews to worship the Phoenician god instead of the true God of
the Israelites.

"Jezebel" is the animal soul that has control of the animal nature. Zeal acts through the soul quality.

To commit fornication or adultery is to mix thoughts, to get two lines of thoughts into action. The animal soul is connected with the animal nature; it also becomes connected with the spiritual, and the individual becomes zealous for both the sense and the spiritual. This is adultery (MD 654).

We are admonished to turn from such ("repent of her doings"), and hold fast to spiritual ideals. Unless this reformation is forthcoming the law will operate to bring dire results ("I am he who searches mind and heart, and I will give to each one of you as your works deserve").

"He who conquers and who keeps my works until the end, I will give him power over the nations, and he shall rule them with a rod of iron . . . and I will give him the morning star" (Rev. 2:26).

In rising above the sensuousness of the human self and directing our zeal toward doing the works of God, we develop the spiritual perception and understanding that enable us to gain and maintain control over the forces of our being ("rule them [the nations] with a rod of iron"). The morning star is symbolic of the Christ ideal which we can attain, and in making it our own it shines beauty and light upon us.

Read Chapter 3:1-6. The angel of the fifth church, Sardis, is addressed as "him who has the seven spirits of God and the seven stars." This is Christ as master of the natural or sense man. Sardis symbolizes "riches of power . . . also joyous dominion" (MD 574). The dominion the Creator gave us is meant to be exercised over ourself, and we can claim it by rising above the desires of our lower nature. The mortal consciousness is like a child that needs discipline and training. Apropos to this Charles Fillmore says:

> We are developing the sevenfold man of the stars. There is no limit to what we can become. Not only may we control and direct and use our own faculties, but we can use the spiritual powers and propensities. If we allow our thoughts of power to slow down, however, we lose the spiritual aspect of power. . . . When we get angry, excited, or confused, cross currents enter our consciousness and we cannot get into the silence, we cannot get in touch with the spiritual. We should affirm power and dominion (MD 574).

The human desire is for dominion over other people and outer conditions. For a time it may seem that we succeed but, actually, we succeed only in deceiving ourself. Christ is not deceived ("I know your works; you have the name of being alive, and you are dead"). Be on the alert and strengthen the spiritual aspect of power, else the divine law will deprive us of it ("I will come like a thief, and you will not know at what hour I will come upon you"). However, once our spiritual development has begun, we are never again wholly involved in negation ("you have still a few names in Sardis, people who have not soiled their garments"), and this spiritual residue helps us to return to Christ ("they shall walk with me in white, for they are worthy").

> "He who conquers shall be clad thus in white garments, and I will not blot his name out of the book of life; I will confess his name before my Father and before his angels" (Rev. 3:5).

White raiment represents the purity that clothes us as we move from the mortal to the spiritual aspect of power. The book of life is the permanent record of our spiritual advancement which cannot be erased. Whatever we have developed in ourself that is like Spirit is recognized or "confessed" by our own Christ self.

Read Chapter 3:7-13. The angel of the sixth church, Philadelphia, is addressed as "the holy one, the true one, who has the key of David, who opens and no one shall shut, who shuts and no one opens." This is Christ as spiritual love, which is irresistible in its action. David, a type of Christ, represents divine love individualized in the soul. To have the "key of David" means to be able to express love in its highest aspect. Philadelphia, meaning brotherly love, also stands for the love center (MD 523).

In our present state of development we express both the divine and human aspects of love. The former is the worthy activity of love and is shown by our obedience to Christ and by our acknowledgment of His presence ("You have kept my word and have not denied my name"). Human love, which has much of selfishness in it, often masquerades under the guise of spiritual love ("those . . . who say that they are Jews and are not, but lie"). Christ detects this duplicity and makes human love subservient to divine love ("I will make them come and bow down before your feet, and learn that I have loved you").

Because of our faithfulness, we receive the assurance that Christ will come to our aid in times of stress ("I am coming soon"). He cautions us to retain the blessings God has given us ("hold fast what you have, so that no one may seize your crown"). Our crown is the symbol of our divinity and its jewels are the spiritual qualities God has bestowed upon us. A crown also indicates authority. We have the authority not to permit any person or condition to deprive us of the love we have from Him. We must hold to it for only love can harmonize every situation that arises.

> "He who conquers, I will make him a pillar in the temple of my God; never shall he go out of it, and I will write on him the name of my God, and the name of the city of my God, the New Jerusalem which comes down from my God out of heaven, and my own new name" (Rev. 3:12).

With spiritual love at the helm of our being we become like a pillar, strong and immovable, in the house of the Lord. No more do we "go out" into error thinking and feeling, and therefore there is no need for the soul to reincarnate ("never shall he go out of it"). Love is truly the "fulfilling of the law," and it is the name of all that is Godlike.

Read Chapter 3:14-22. The angel of the seventh and last church, Laodicea, is addressed as "the Amen, the faithful and true witness, the beginnning of God's creation." This is Christ as ultimate truth. Laodicea represents "a phase of the judgment faculty in the individual, expressing in the personal. It is that phase of judgment which bases its understanding, its decisions, on outer seemings and intellectual reasonings" (MD 395).

If we vacillate between human reason and divine judgment our mind is divided and has no stability ("because you are lukewarm, and neither cold nor hot, I will spew you out of my mouth"). Separated from the source of wisdom, we become increasingly worldly-minded and fall into the error of thinking that we are sufficient unto ourself ("I am rich, I have prospered, and I need nothing"). The belief that outer prosperity is all we need kills any desire for the inner wealth that flows from the realization of God as our abundance. This is an exceedingly dangerous state of mind for "apart from me you can do nothing" (John 15:5), says the Christ. John's advice to us is to seek spiritual treasure ("buy from me gold refined by fire"), purity ("white garments to clothe you"), and spiritual insight ("salve to anoint your eyes, that you may see").

This is the one state of consciousness (church) that warrants rebuke and draws no commendation from Christ. Nevertheless, He still loves the erring soul, counsels repentance and offers forgiveness ("Behold, I stand at the door and knock; if any one

hears my voice and opens the door, I will come in to
him and eat with him, and he with me"). We have but
to open the door of our heart to Him. He is always
there and always ready to respond.

> "He who conquers, I will grant him to sit with me on
> my throne, as I myself conquered and sat down with
> my Father on his throne" (Rev. 3:21).

The ultimate truth is that God and man are unified in Christ. The great intercessory prayer of Jesus,
"as thou, Father, art in me, and I in thee, that they
also may be in us" (John 17:21), is answered when
we rise above the mistaken belief that we have no
need of Him. By our acceptance of Christ, we share
in His glory ("sit with me on my throne").

Each of the seven messages contain this one
specific instruction: "He who has an ear, let him hear
what the Spirit says to the churches." The ability to
hear is born of our faithfulness in prayer and our
eagerness to be receptive to His word. Spirit will
direct every step of our way if we hear and heed.
Only His word obeyed will enable us to overcome
the "sin which clings so closely" (Heb. 12:1), and
continue on the path of spiritual unfoldment.

The New Birth

Revelation 4–11

We are now ready to begin the study of the main
section of Revelation, which consists of the six
visions contained in chapters four through twenty.
This lesson considers three of the visions.

At this point it is well to remember that the book
makes it clear that this is the revelation of Jesus
Christ to the disciple or initiate (John). Therefore it
is only for the person who has begun his conscious
spiritual development. Mankind is gradually progressing in every department of his life but in the
earlier stages of his evolution, his interests remain
almost exclusively in the personal self and the outer
world. The day comes, however, when he hears the
voice of the Lord, "Out of Egypt have I called my
son," and he yearns to know his Creator. This desire
gradually replaces the longing for the things of the
world, and his attention becomes focused on the
spiritual realm. His attitude is very different from
that of the person with only a superficial interest in
religion. Jesus said, "Blessed are those who hunger
and thirst for righteousness, for they shall be satisfied." It is when the desire to know God becomes
intense that the aspirant seeks His kingdom with
singleness of purpose and persistence. Only then can
the spiritual infilling begin. It always does so with
the soul quickening which follows a perception of
the presence of the Son of God (Rev. 1).

The tutoring of the initiate by his indwelling Christ starts with the instructions given in the letters to the seven churches. They disclose that the soul is divided between the virtues the initiate has developed and the faults he has allowed to remain or has taken on from the race thought. Though every soul contains both good and bad qualities, these are not well defined in the average person, and there is only a superficial tussle when conscience goes contrary to personal desire. But when the soul is set for spiritual enlightenment, the inner conflict becomes severe. The initiate can no longer believe in both light and darkness, or "the spirit of truth and the spirit of error" (I John 4:6). He has chosen to follow Christ and to do so he must expel the belief in evil. This gives rise to the inner struggles to which every aspirant is subjected. Progressing from double vision (seeing good and evil) to single vision (seeing God only) is spiritual mastery.

The six visions record the battles within the soul as the initiate moves forward. He is aware of the Christ power but also of the power of the Antichrist. Both *seem* so real to him. The visions present tests that enable him to discern the deceptiveness of evil and to realize the allness of God.

"Man, know thyself," says the voice of wisdom. The visions are self-revealing. Through the ages the soul has lived at various times on earth, it has built up, in ignorance of God, a self apart from Him. This shadow self is the sense or carnal consciousness, and it has brought sin, sickness, and death to mankind.

By a series of terrifying visions, Revelation exposes this consciousness and uncovers hidden facets of thought and feeling that the initiate may be reluctant to admit (or may not even be aware of). In studying them it should always be kept in mind that they deal with states of consciousness. They have no relation whatsoever to actual people or to outer conditions.

Throughout the first three visions the initiate is fighting somewhat blindly. Yet even in despair he calls upon God and therefore is never completely overcome by adverse forces.

"The name of the LORD is a strong tower;
   the righteous man runs into it and is safe"
(Prov. 18:10).

This is exactly what the initiate does. By calling on the name of the Lord he gains enough strength to meet the next test. There can be no failure for the one who sets his mind to reach the kingdom prepared for him since the dawn of creation.

First Vision — God's Throne and the Lamb
Revelation 4, 5

This vision begins the complicated symbolism that is often difficult for the modern scholar to interpret. Yet for those who believe that Revelation deals with man's spiritual unfoldment the vast majority of the symbols are understandable, and the reader is intrigued by the fascinating story they unfold.

As the first instructions to the initiate (letters to churches) come as a result of his vision of the Christ, so the tests that lie before him are the outgrowth of his vision of the heavenly realm. A spiritual rhythm is established in the prologue which operates throughout the book. The initiate moves in and out of spiritual consciousness, rising to a high state of realization and then dropping back to the human level of thought. It will be noted that the difficulties the initiate meets are invariably induced by a spiritual realization and followed by one.

Read Chapter 4. We have prepared the way for this vision by abiding by the instructions given in the letters. Now we are ready to take a step forward. This is offered by the invitation, "Come up hither, and I will show you what must take place after this." We rise in consciousness and perceive things as they are on the inner plane ("in heaven an open door"). Everything that we see with the inner eye proclaims the Shekinah or glory of the Almighty—the throne, jewels, rainbow, sea of glass, et cetera. The accumulation of power is represented by the twenty-four elders and the four living creatures who are round about the throne. The number twelve (signifying perfection) is used for the first time, and the multiple of twelve specified here and elsewhere in Revelation denotes the presence of a mighty spiritual force. The white robes worn by the elders represent purity and the crowns stand for authority.

The four living creatures described as "full of eyes in front and behind," and with six wings, signify the ability of Spirit to see all and to soar to heavenly realms. These creatures were described in the first chapter of Ezekiel. The prophet describes them as having the face of a man, a lion, an ox, and an eagle. They are considered as identical with the cherubim, a high order of angels. In the traditions of both Babylonia and Egypt, the cherubim were represented by the lion, bull, eagle, and angel. The symbolism was perpetuated in the mysterious Sphinx. In Hebrew scripture the cherubim were generally indicative of God's presence but were also thought of as the guardians of sacred things. It was the cherubim who protected the tree of life in the Garden of Eden, and who stretched their wings over the place of the Ark in the Temple. Charles Fillmore states, "the cherubim are symbolic figures representing the attributes and majesty of God" (RW 33).

Both the twenty-four elders and the four living creatures are invariably present at times of illumination for the initiate. They are indicative of the spiritual outpouring from on high that we receive when we are conscious of the Christ presence.

The purpose of the vision is to arouse in us adoration for God and acknowledgment of Him:

"Holy, holy, holy, is the Lord God Almighty,
    who was and is and is to come!

Read Chapter 5. Following this exalted period of consciousness, we drop back to our usual level of thought and realize there is much about Him that we do not understand (He holds a scroll which is "sealed with seven seals"). Neither our highest perception of truth (angel) nor any person can reveal Him to us, and we are distressed ("wept much that no one was found worthy to open the scroll"). God is known only to His Son, Jesus Christ, who is described both as the Lion of the tribe of Judah, and as the Lamb "standing, as though it had been slain." The Hebrew prophets had foretold a Messiah who would be of the line of David, and it was their custom to sacrifice a lamb without blemish unto the Lord. The crucifixion of Jesus identifies Him with the Lamb. Only Christ has full understanding and authority (Lamb with "seven horns and with seven eyes"). He is willing to act in our behalf and disclose the mystery of God ("he took the scroll from the right hand of him who was seated on the throne").

At this we are overjoyed and elevated by the spiritual forces flowing from Him (elders, living creatures, and angels), and we sing a "new song" in adoration of God and His Son ("to him who sits upon the throne and to the Lamb be blessing and honor and glory and might for ever and ever!"). The idea of a new song comes from the Psalms: "O sing to the LORD a new song" (Psalms 96:1). The song is always a paean of praise and is used in Revelation at those times when the initiate is overwhelmingly aware of the divine Presence.

Second Vision — The Seven-Sealed Book
Revelation 6—8:1

Read Chapter 6. This vision is a continuation of
the former one and tells what takes place in our
consciousness as more of God's truth is revealed
(seven seals opened). Four strong beliefs which we
have at this stage of our development are represented
by four horsemen. The first to be revealed (opening
of first seal) is the Christ (rider of the white horse
who "went out conquering and to conquer"). We
have already acknowledged Him and have faith in
His power to conquer all obstacles. This faith is to be
rewarded at a later time. But we are also harboring
three very destructive beliefs inherited from the race
consciousness and we are still bound by them now.
These are shown with the opening of the next three
seals.

As the three horsemen parade before us we perceive the disastrous effects they have produced in
our life. One is war (rider of the red horse). Along
with the majority of mankind, we continue to believe that we must fight for what we want, or else
fight to protect what we have. War, between nations
or individuals, can never secure our right for it is
contrary to God's law of love and cooperation. War
is conflict and so long as we have dissenting elements
in our mind, there can be no peace within or without.

Another firmly entrenched belief is in famine or
lack (rider of the black horse, bargaining for grain).

It is belief in lack that produces lack. There is no limitation in God's world for He "knows that you need . . . all [these things]" (Matt. 6:32), and has provided them in abundant measure. But He tells us to look to Him for them. When we fail to do so the specter of lack dogs our footsteps.

Still another fixed belief is in death (rider of the pale horse whose "rider's name was Death"). Death is the penalty for living apart from our Lord. When we learn to pattern our life after Him, the last enemy shall be overcome. The sad fact is that we experience many deaths before the body ceases to function. We are dead to health when in sickness, dead to peace when inharmony reigns, and dead to joy when our hearts are bowed down with grief.

These three false beliefs do their part in depriving us of the fullness of life designed by God for His children, and inflict great harm on the self (have power "to kill with sword, and with famine, and with pestilence and by wild beasts of the earth").

The opening of the fifth seal shows the suffering of the soul that is in bondage to these race beliefs (three horsemen). They have overcome us for the time being and our consciousness feels oppressed ("slain for the word of God"). Why should we who are making a conscientious effort to obey Him have to endure such persecution? When will it end ("O Sovereign Lord, holy and true, how long before thou wilt judge and avenge our blood on those who dwell on the earth")? A great cry for release surges up in us but our pain is eased by the realization that our Lord is caring for us. Divine protection is symbolized by the white robes we are given to wear, and He tells us to be at peace ("rest a little longer").

As the revelation of truth continues (sixth seal opened), our mind is thrown into turmoil ("there was a great earthquake"). This word is used frequently to denote an upheaval in consciousness which, on this occasion, is due to a disruption of forces that we have always considered completely stable. What is more reliable than the orderly course of nature? Nevertheless, the physical world can undergo a change ("sun became black ... moon became like blood ... stars ... fell to the earth"). A great truth we have to learn is that outer things have no permanence regardless of how durable they seem nor for how long a time they have functioned. God is the only enduring reality and He is the source of all benefits that come to us from the physical plane. "Look unto Me" is the divine command.

At this stage of our unfoldment the mortal self is terrified when our outer world seems to fall apart. We try to escape the devastation ("hid in the caves and among the rocks of the mountains"). Surely God is angry with us. Who is able to withstand the "wrath of the Lamb"?

Read Chapter 7 and first verse of Chapter 8. The harm we fear is to be nullified by a spiritual agency ("another angel ascend from the rising of the sun"). Angels stand for spiritual ideas active in consciousness. They are powerful and work in our behalf. Now a spiritual idea reveals that we ("servants of our

God") will not be subjected to further trials until we have gained adequate inner strength to cope with them ("sealed . . . upon their foreheads"). "The forehead is the center of consciousness which Truth seals; that is, it secretly unites the consciousness with Christ" (JC 152).

Even a temporary union with Christ increases our spiritual stamina, symbolized by the one hundred and forty-four thousand who are sealed. This figure, a multiple of the perfect number twelve, signifies full or complete protection. We are aware not only of this but also of the fact that there are untold numbers of souls on the spiritual path with us ("a great multitude which no man could number, from every nation"). We are not alone in our devotion to God nor in our struggle for spiritual mastery. With us are those who have made mighty overcomings ("come out of the great tribulation; they have washed their robes and made them white in the blood of the Lamb"). " 'The blood of the Lamb' represents the primal life of Being, which Jesus made accessible to all those who believe in Him as the revealer of the pure life of God the Father" (JC 152).

Again we have soared in consciousness and found our spiritual footing. We understand that our good only expresses through the physical; its origin is Christ.

"For the Lamb in the midst of the throne will be
        their shepherd,
and he will guide them to springs of living water;

and God will wipe away every tear from their eyes".

Note that after each of the tests the visions present, the initiate reaches a spiritual level of thought and praises God. This indicates that he has overcome the deficiencies revealed by the vision and is prepared to continue on his spiritual way. There is no indication of a time element but we know from experience that sometimes we travel rapidly toward our spiritual goal and sometimes we move at a snail's pace. Yet no matter how long it takes us to conquer negative states of mind, this must be done before the next test is presented.

The opening of the seventh seal, in chapter eight, brings a blessed sense of quietness and peace ("There was silence in heaven for about half an hour"). After Jesus overcame the tempter in the wilderness "angels came and ministered to him" (Matt. 4:11). Following the turbulence through which we have passed there is need for time to be still and let what we have learned sink into the soul.

Because we have set ourself for the attainment of the Christ consciousness, *all* in us that is unlike God must be eliminated. An opportunity for additional purification is soon on its way and having put our hand to the plow, we cannot turn back.

Third Vision — The Seven Trumpets
Revelation 8:2-11

A trumpet is blown to proclaim an important message from one in authority to those who are to carry out its provisions. The blast of a trumpet is loud and clear, demanding attention, and the use of the word here is to inform us that what we are to hear is of great moment. Starting with this vision the inner conflicts between the spiritual and mortal consciousness become more severe. Jesus said, "Do not think that I have come to bring peace on earth; I have not come to bring peace, but a sword" (Matt. 10:34). The truth He gave is like a sword that slashes at our mortal concepts and they resist with all their might. The ensuing battle is a fierce one.

Read Chapter 8. At first glance it seems strange that angels blow the trumpets which bring disasters. Angels are spiritual ideas, "our perceptive faculties, which ever dwell in the presence of the Father" (MD 52). Each of us has an angel self that is made up of all the spiritual thoughts and aspirations we have ever had, and it is through our angels (thoughts) that Christ speaks to us. But can spiritual ideas ever bring trials? Indeed, yes. They uncover false beliefs and it is by meeting and conquering these that our soul is emancipated. So, though it may seem that what our angels show us about ourself is quite unpleasant, the revelation is a blessing. They expose defects of which we are unaware. However, our reason tells us we have many shortcomings and when we are earnest in our

desire to be like Him, we cry:
>"But who can discern his errors?
>   Clear thou me from hidden faults"
>
>   *(Psalms 19:12).*

Our prayer is answered by spiritual ideas (angels) which bring these to light.

The peaceful consciousness attained at the end of the second vision is still with us as the third vision begins (the angel "stood at the altar" with a censer and incense to which was added the prayers of the saints). The time has arrived for us to bring our heavenly thoughts into expression (angel took the censer, "filled it with fire from the altar and threw it on the earth"). There followed "thunders, loud noises, flashes of lightning, and an earthquake." This phrase is used often in Revelation when the initiate is in a high state of consciousness. It denotes the cleansing power of Spirit which fits him for the experiences that lie ahead.

The sounding of the first four trumpets causes devastating conditions to appear in our outer life, symbolized by (1) "hail and fire . . . fell on the earth"; (2) "a great mountain, burning with fire was thrown into the sea"; (3) a great star, called Wormwood, fell into the rivers and poisoned them; (4) sun, moon, and stars were darkened.

It is the belief in the reality of misfortune that must be erased, and by now we have made some progress in this direction. When the sixth seal was opened (Chapter 6:12-17) and our faith in the outer world was put to the test, we were frightened and greatly upset. But we turned quickly to God and were given divine protection. However, the belief itself still remains, and the sounding of the four trumpets brings us face to face with it again. By now we have grown in spiritual understanding and perceive that earthly trials can affect only a small area of our being, a third part. This represents that portion of the sense consciousness which clings to limitation as a reality. The greater part of our being, the Christ self, is untouched.

Though this realization shows that we have taken a long step forward, the battle over mortal consciousness is far from being won. Our human beliefs ("those who dwell on the earth") will encounter additional trials of a similar nature. This is depicted by the eagle, a symbol of doom, flying in midheaven and crying, "Woe, woe, woe."

Read Chapter 9:1-11. As the fifth trumpet is sounded, some of the violent and cruel emotions of the carnal nature are exposed. These are buried deep in the subconscious mind ("shaft of the bottomless pit"), and blacken our soul ("the sun and the air were darkened with the smoke from the shaft"). We have little conception of the extent of the damage they cause and are usually loath even to admit their presence in us. When they are brought to our attention we are likely to make light of them or dismiss them as harmless (like locusts, which are destructive pests but not dangerous). We fail to realize that they are venomous (like the poisonous sting of scorpions).

These vicious elements in the subconscious do not have complete control over us for we have gained a measure of spirituality ("the seal of God"). But when they rise to the surface of consciousness as feelings of hate, revenge, envy, or the like, they cause us great pain for the time they are allowed to express (torment us for "five months"). Our pain is so severe that we feel unable to stand it and beg for a release that does not come ("they will long to die, and death will fly from them").

A picture of the repulsiveness of these emotions flashes before us (the locusts are like horses prepared for war, with men's faces, women's hair, and lions' teeth). They are well protected (armed with "iron breastplates"), and we finally see them for what they really are: demonic powers that can poison us (have scorpions' tails). Their name is Destruction (Abaddon or Apollyon).

With this revelation the first woe is past.

Read Chapter 9:13-21. This section of the vision pinpoints the evil of idolatry. Our strongest spiritual idea (angel who blows the sixth trumpet) gathers other spiritual ideas ("release[s] the four angels who are bound"), and attacks the belief in idols and partially destroys it ("kill[s] a third of mankind"). When the first four trumpets were sounded (Chapter 8:7-12), it was specified that the trials reached "a third," meaning a portion of the carnal thought. Here the same term is used, indicating that this thought is gradually being undermined as one after another of its defects is paraded before the initiate.

The carnal mind in its entirety is not destroyed until the end of the sixth vision. Though we wish it could be disposed of in one fell swoop, we are beginning to understand that the purification of the soul is a gradual process requiring of us great faith in God and infinite patience with ourself.

Our spiritual self rises to do battle with the mortal. The forces of the former are numerous ("the number of the troops of cavalry was twice ten thousand times ten thousand"); they are well-protected ("riders wore breastplates the color of fire"), and they are powerful ("the heads of the horses were like lions' heads"). Some of the idolatrous beliefs are slain by them, but some escape, and they remain unchanged ("did not repent of the works of their hands"), and continue to worship all manner of false gods ("demons and idols of gold and silver and bronze and stone and wood, which cannot either see or hear or walk").

Sense thoughts are deeply imbedded in our mind, and though they are the cause of much of our suffering, we refuse to relinquish them. The worship of idols is one of our cardinal sins. The second commandment reads, "You shall not make for yourself a graven image," but on the whole this is consistently ignored by mankind. As long as the human ego, or personality, or wealth, or ambition, or pleasure holds sway over us, we are making a graven image. Jesus said: "You shall worship the Lord your God and him only shall you serve" (Matt. 4:10). When we worship anything less than God, we are guilty of idolatry. This is the root of sin and its offspring, immorality and crime ("nor did they repent of their murders or their sorceries or their immorality or their thefts").

Read Chapter 10. Before the seventh trumpet is sounded the initiate needs time to learn and assimilate more of Truth. The revelations that come to him in this chapter and the following one (through 11:14), are to assist him in this. The divine law is one of love and never puts more upon us than we are able to bear.

The description of the angel who gives this message is filled with spiritual symbols such as are generally used in connection with Christ, thus showing that he represents a powerful spiritual idea (wrapped with a cloud, a rainbow over his head, "his face was like the sun, and his legs like pillars of fire"). Additional understanding of God is to be given us (angel "had a little scroll open in his hand"), and our attention is emphatically called to it ("called out with a loud voice, like a lion roaring"). A delay to our investigation is caused by "seven thunders."

Verses 3 and 4 are obscure. One Bible reference is to Psalm 29:3-9, in which the voice of the Lord thunders seven times proclaiming His greatness. Here the most likely meaning seems to be that the seven thunders predict another series of tests which do, in fact, come. We are cautioned not to speak of this, but our angel insists that there is to be no delay and that before the tests (and with the sounding of the seventh trumpet) God's purpose will be revealed ("the mystery of God . . . should be fulfilled").

We are to assimilate the divine word (take the little scroll and eat it). It will be pleasant to the taste but most unpleasant to digest. This proves to be true ("it was sweet as honey in my mouth, but when I had eaten it my stomach was made bitter"). How well we know this! When the wonders of the spiritual realm are first disclosed to us we are enchanted. New, exciting, and inspiring vistas open to our mind and heart. Yet when we learn more and discover that truth is contrary to many of our cherished opinions, what was once sweet becomes bitter. The most difficult of all things is to put Truth principles into practice. Nevertheless, we are to keep trying and are instructed to speak the word diligently ("again prophesy about many peoples and nations"). The word is quick and powerful and always strengthens our faith.

Read Chapter 11:1-6. Continuing the process of learning more about God and His law, we are told to evaluate our spiritual consciousness ("measure the temple of God and the altar and those who worship there"). In explanation of this Charles Fillmore says:

> Things are sometimes measured to find out not their size, but their true value. The Temple was in Jerusalem and represents the place of worship in the heart center. . . . The altar would be the consciousness of full consecration that takes place first in the Temple of worship. . . . "Them that worship therein" are the true spiritual thoughts in man that love and worship God (MD 678).

No attention is to be given to the lower consciousness, though it will function actively for a time (do not measure the outer court "for it is given over to the nations, and they will trample over the holy city for forty-two months"):

> Those who are in the process of overcoming realize that . . . within them are the carnal mind, or the outer, personal self, and the inner or Christ consciousness of Truth. The putting off of the personal is a gradual work, which begins after a full consecration to God on the part of the individual, and until it is entirely overcome there is often "war in heaven" within him. So the "court which is without the temple" that "hath been given unto the nations," and was not to be measured, represents the carnal thoughts or states of consciousness, conscious and subconscious, that have not yet been redeemed. Until they are lifted up and redeemed they to a certain extent "tread under foot," or keep from perfect expression and demonstration, the spirituality or God consciousness within man (MD 678).

There is always at hand a spiritual power to counteract evil and the Lord provides an advocate for us ("I will grant my two witnesses power to prophesy for one thousand two hundred and sixty days"). Note that this time is equal to that of the forty-two months of the Adversary's work, and indicated a cancellation of it. The symbolism of the two witnesses is taken from Zechariah. When the prophet asked who they were, the Lord replied, "Not by might, nor by power, but by my Spirit, says the LORD of hosts" (Zech. 4:6). In other words, the two witnesses were emissaries of God. Here they denote the same superhuman activity ("have power to shut the sky, that no rain may fall . . . to turn them [the waters] into blood, and to smite the earth with every plague"). How often we have seen an exhibition of spiritual might working for us in what seemed to be a miraculous way!

Read Chapter 11:7-14. Being unable to sustain spiritual consciousness indefinitely, we revert to mortal thought. The latter is represented by "the beast that ascends from the bottomless pit." Mortal thought has sufficient strength to contend with and overthrow the spiritual ("the beast . . . will make war upon them [two witnesses] and conquer them and kill them"). There is nothing unusual about an experience of this kind. The Bible records a number of instances where the sense self is victorious over the spiritual, but it is always made clear that the spiritual is revived. The allegory of Cain, Abel, and Seth is an example. Though Cain slew Abel, Seth was born and took Abel's place.

The sense self rejoices for truth torments it ("those who dwell on the earth will . . . make merry"), but its joy is short-lived; for after a brief period, our higher consciousness is reanimated (two witnesses are resurrected after "three and a half days"). We hear the command of Christ, "Come up higher!" and again rise to spiritual heights ("went up to heaven"). Our sense consciousness is violently shaken and another portion of it is destroyed ("there was a great earthquake, and a tenth of the city fell"). Awed by this display of God-power with us, we praise Him ("gave glory to the God of heaven").

The second woe is now past.

Read Chapter 11:15-19. The time has finally come for the sounding of the seventh trumpet. It has been revealed to us that when this takes place "the mystery of God . . . should be fulfilled" (10:7). We have come a long way since this revelation. God's word is clearer to us (we have eaten the little scroll) and we have seen that the mortal can be overcome by the spiritual (two witnesses resurrected). A cycle of soul development has been completed. We are aware of this and are exuberant.

When the seventh seal was opened (8:1), it brought a feeling of inward quietness, but the sounding of the seventh trumpet brings a profound realization that Christ is Lord of all ("the kingdom of the world has become the kingdom of our Lord . . . and he shall reign for ever and ever"). We are grateful that His rule is a just one ("we give thanks to thee, Lord God Almighty . . . that thou hast taken thy great power and begun to reign. . . . Came . . . the time . . . for rewarding thy servants . . . and for destroying the destroyers of the earth"). Once again we are aware that the cleansing of our soul is continuing ("there were flashes of lightning, loud noises, peals of thunder, an earthquake, and heavy hail").

The third woe is now past.

The New Birth

Revelation 12–18

The two visions contained in this lesson represent the most difficult phases of the initiate's spiritual development. He has gained sufficient understanding of God to substantiate his faith to a marked degree and is becoming increasingly aware of the Christ presence and power. Yet he is also aware of and feels the tremendous pressure of the sense consciousness. He tries to hold to Christ but finds it well-nigh impossible to escape the clutches of those beliefs that are so much a part of him. He has reached the place where he neither can nor will retreat, and he is left alone like Jacob to wrestle with his higher self until the break of day. Holding on despite pain he cries, "I will not let you go, unless you bless me" (Gen. 32:26).

Fourth Vision - The Woman and the Dragon

Revelation 12–14

Recognition of the supremacy of the spiritual, "We give thanks to thee, Lord God Almighty . . . that thou hast taken thy great power and begun to reign" (11:17), upholds us for the experiences that are to follow. The sense consciousness has great power, the power given it by our faith and acknowledgment. The fourth vision reveals the consciousness in all its ugliness. No longer is it to be hid; it is now to be brought out into the open.

Read Chapter 12:1-12. The woman "clothed with the sun, with the moon under her feet, and on her head a crown of twelve stars" represents the purified soul, or the soul that has been cleansed by giving its attention to the Lord and being obedient to His word. Of the woman Charles Fillmore says:

> Inherent within man are both the masculine and feminine principles; when this fact is realized there is a union of the two. Of this union is born the regenerate life. The 12th chapter of Revelation pertains to man in the stage of spiritual development in which he has recognized this truth to the extent that he is enabled to "express" or to bring forth. The woman symbolizes this individual—the soul—clothed in Spirit (the sun). The moon (intellect, to which physical birth is subject), is beneath her feet. The twelve stars are the twelve centers of consciousness, concentrated at the one head, I.

When we attain this state of enlightenment we are aware of carrying within us a divine life which must be brought forth. This is no easy thing to do ("she cried out in her pangs of birth, in anguish for delivery"). Opposing the soul (woman) are all the degenerate forces in us that make up the carnal self, represented by the "great red dragon." He is described as having "seven heads and ten horns," and Charles Fillmore states:

The dragon means the personal or mortal self, and the seven heads are the seven ruling desires of this self. The ten horns are the five intellectual faculties doubled, because every faculty is dual and at war with itself.

When the soul finally gives birth to its highest conception of the Christ (child is born), the carnal self (dragon) seeks to destroy the Holy One (intends to devour the child). But evil can never destroy good ("child was caught up to God"), and the soul is protected ("woman fled into the wilderness, where she has a place prepared by God"). This place is the inner closet or lofty state of consciousness where the soul is free from stress and is nourished by Spirit.

"Now war arose in heaven." Heaven represents spiritual realization and when attacked by the sense mind, the resulting inner strife is severe (Michael and his angels warred with the dragon and his allies). Our spiritual consciousness proves to be stronger than the mortal and overcomes the adversary ("the great dragon was thrown down" from heaven). The true nature of the sense consciousness is now revealed. Its name is Devil and Satan, and it is the "deceiver of the whole world." The race belief is that there are two powers operative in human life, God and Devil. Here we are shown that God alone has reality. The only power the carnal mind has is what we give it by our destructive thoughts and emotions. It holds us in bondage until we see it for what it is, the great deceiver. Cast out of the heaven of our mind, it shall no longer be able to exercise the influence we once gave it.

This realization brings great rejoicing and we hastily declare our loyalty to the One ("now the salvation and the power and the kingdom of our God and the authority of his Christ have come").

We have now reached a crisis in our unfoldment. We know what is true and what is false, and though we do not have the spiritual strength to expel all our error beliefs and they continue to plague us, we are never again completely duped by them.

Read Chapter 12:13-17. Recognizing the unreality of the sense consciousness is a vital step forward, but it is quite a different matter to be free of it. The realization that it is a sham comes to the highest level of the mind, the superconsciousness, but it must be accepted by the entire consciousness. Our inmost self knows that God is supreme (victory gained in heaven), yet there still remains the problem of dealing with evil in outer manifestation (on earth). The carnal self has not been destroyed, only "thrown down," and it is determined to regain its control over the soul ("he pursued the woman who had borne the male child"). We are protected by Spirit ("given the two wings of the great eagle that she [the woman] might fly . . . to the place where she is to be nourished"). But the carnal self is determined, and contrives ingenious ways to satisfy its desires ("The serpent poured water like a river out of his mouth after the woman, to sweep her away with the flood"). Divine Mind also is ingenious and functions through unusual agencies to protect its own ("the earth opened its mouth and swallowed the river which the dragon had poured from his mouth"). Frustrated, the carnal self ceases its direct attack and works slyly to undermine the soul ("the dragon was angry with the woman, and went off to make war on the rest of her offspring").

Read Chapter 13:1-10. The sense consciousness (dragon) now selects a particularly abominable ally, represented by "a beast rising out of the sea." The beast is connected with the dragon for he too has "ten horns and seven heads." He is likewise treacherous and dangerous ("like a leopard, its feet were like a bear's, and its mouth was like a lion's mouth"), and his strength is derived from the dragon ("to it the dragon gave his power and his throne and great authority"). We have encountered this bestial state of consciousness before and were temporarily defeated, but we finally overcame it. (See account of the two witnesses and the beast in Chapter 11:7-11.) The wound we inflicted has now healed and here is this destructive belief again, honored by those worldly thoughts in us that fear its power ("they worshiped the beast, saying, 'Who is like the beast, and who can fight against it?' ").

The beast is a type of the Antichrist and denotes that phase of the carnal consciousness that reviles the Lord ("it opened its mouth to utter blasphemies against God"). The word *blasphemy* has several meanings, the most general of which is to speak irreverently of God or curse Him. In the opinion of the Jews, Jesus blasphemed by calling Himself the Son of God. In Truth, we consider blasphemy a violation of the third commandment which reads: "You shall not take the name of the Lord your God in vain; for the Lord will not hold him guiltless who takes his name in vain" (Exod. 20:7). This is interpreted to mean that we are guilty of blasphemy by connecting anything of a negative character with Him. "I AM" is our spiritual identity, it is God's name in us—and we are taking His name in vain when we say "I am sick," or poor, or weak, and so on.

Blasphemy also takes the form of rejecting the Almighty ("it [the beast] was allowed to make war on the saints and to conquer them"). Atheists frankly deny that there is a Supreme Being. "The fool says in his heart, 'There is no God' " (Psalms 14:1), and man is indeed foolish in thinking that the wonders of creation are not the result of a wisdom far surpassing what he has attained or can attain. But the average person who claims to believe in God, in actual practice does not consider Him the most important part of his life. He may actually attribute many of his hardships to Him: "It is God's will," he says. Even the sincere devotee often doubts whether God is mindful of him and will direct his way. These are forms of blasphemy which revile the Lord in a subtle manner by withholding from the Almighty the recognition and adoration due Him ("all who dwell on earth will worship it [beast], every one whose name has not been written in the book of life of the Lamb").

It is most helpful to have this evil brought to our attention for it must be consciously expelled.

Though we cannot as yet fully control the unregenerate state of mind which continues to indulge in blasphemy (worship the beast), our higher self is aware of it and understands that the divine law brings a penalty for sin

("If any one is to be taken captive,
    to captivity he goes;
if any one slays with the sword,
    with the sword must he be slain").

Read Chapter 13:11-18. We have penetrated the disguise of the error belief typified by the beast out of the sea and its power therefore is lessened, but the carnal mind is not easily defeated. It (dragon) selects another agent, represented by the beast out of the earth, also called the false prophet (16:13, 19:20). Its character is cleverly concealed and at first glance, it appears to be quite innocuous ("it had two horns like a lamb"). However, its affiliation with the dragon is soon revealed ("it spoke like a dragon" and "makes the earth and its inhabitants worship the first beast").

The erroneous states of mind symbolized by the two beasts are closely connected. The first beast denotes the sacrilegious consciousness that blasphemes God. The second beast represents the belief that human might is superior to divine might. Together they give verification to the adage that "birds of a feather flock together." Both are untrue, malicious, and do us great harm.

The false prophet is capable of performing wondrous feats which are considered the prerogative of spiritually illumined souls ("it works great signs, even making fire come down from heaven to earth in the sight of men"). Wisdom is often required to discriminate between spiritual power and human ability. Many marvelous achievements are made by those functioning only on the intellectual plane. Jesus' sage remark, "The sons of this world are wiser in their own generation than the sons of light" (Luke 16:8), brings to mind the fact that the person who is expressing in the personal knows the rules of the world and abides by them; whereas the spiritual aspirant is torn between the spiritual and the human and is unable to give his full support to either. His consciousness is thus divided and little is accomplished.

However, such is an inevitable stage of our unfoldment. It is impossible to move from the human to the spiritual plane in the twinkling of an eye, and for a time we are bound to fluctuate between them. Consequently when the power of the human is exhibited, we are apt to conclude that, after all, it may surpass that of the spiritual. As problems arise we are sorely tempted to depend upon ourself or other people for their solution. While it is certainly true that the Lord often works through human channels, we should never attribute to the human what belongs to God. Such is the false prophet talking to us and implanting the insidious idea that we have no need of God ("by the signs which it is allowed to work . . . it deceives those who dwell on earth").

The belief in the superiority of the human (second beast) renews the consciousness that reviles God (first beast); "it [second beast] was allowed to give breath to the image of the beast," and threatens calamity for refusal to adhere to this belief ("to cause those who would not worship the image of the beast to be slain"). Success is denied those who have not been "marked on their right hand or on the forehead." Spiritual wisdom shows us that this is utterly untenable by revealing the identity of the false prophet ("its number is six hundred and sixty-six"). This figure connects the second beast with the Emperor Nero, the first to persecute Christians. If Neron Caesar is written in Hebrew and the letters given their numerical value, the total is six hundred and sixty-six. Spiritually interpreted, the number stands for that which is in violent opposition to and attempts to slay the spiritual.

Read Chapter 14:1-13. We have been alerted to the deceptiveness of the "mind of the flesh," as Paul calls the carnal self (dragon and two beasts), and our soul is filled with gladness. Christ is very real and with Him is a multitude of divine powers ("I looked, and lo, on Mount Zion stood the Lamb, and with him a hundred and forty-four thousand who had his name and his Father's name written on their foreheads"). We hear the new song which rings strong and clear ("like the sound of many waters"), and know that it can be sung only by those who have shown their devotion to Christ ("follow the Lamb wherever he goes"), and are truthful and pure ("in their mouth no lie was found, for they are spotless").

To this elevated consciousness God's grand purpose is revealed. It is couched in the form of three predictions given through our angel self. While they refer to what shall take place, they are not given in the future tense but in the present tense. This is a reminder that there is no time in Spirit: "That which hath been is now; and that which is to be hath already been" (Eccles. 3:15 A.V.).

These predictions are: (1) Divine judgment is being exercised ("the hour of his [God's] judgment has come"); (2) The power exercised by the material world is doomed to destruction ("Fallen, fallen, is Babylon the great"); (3) The mortal self is rejected by God and suffering is its lot ("if any one worships the beast . . . he also shall drink the wine of God's wrath . . . and he shall be tormented with fire and brimstone . . . and they [the worshipers of the beast] have no rest, day or night").

Assurance is given that those who "die in the Lord" shall be blessed. These words have a twofold meaning. In an outer sense they were intended to give comfort to Christians who were facing martyrdom. Spiritually, they confirm Jesus' promise: "He who loses his life for my sake will find it" (Matt. 10:39). By "dying" to the mortal way of life the door to a fuller existence opens to us.

Read Chapter 14:14-20. By now we have learned many spiritual lessons and understand that the time has come for the outer or conscious self (earth) to be further refined (harvested, or the clusters of the vine gathered). This task is to be undertaken by our spiritual thoughts (angels) that forcibly expel the mortal beliefs (use a sharp sickle). As we well know, these beliefs are stubborn and require of us a firm and positive denial of their reality. To the mortal self it is a painful process when destructive thoughts and emotions are ejected ("threw . . . into the great wine press of the wrath of God"), and suffering is symbolized by the great amount of blood which comes from the grapes as they are trodden in the wine press. Such cleansing is beneficial and we endure as best we can. Later on in our spiritual ongoing it will be revealed to us that there is an easier and more effective way of disposing of undesirable mental states: that is, to "let go and let God."

Fifth Vision - The Seven Bowls

Revelation 15—18

Due to the work that has been done in the soul thus far, we have progressed in understanding and strength. Our great desire is to go forward and finish the course laid out by our Lord, and surely this prayer is on our lips:

"Let the words of my mouth and meditation of
   my heart
  be acceptable in thy sight,
  O Lord, my rock and my redeemer"
(Psalms 19:14).

It cannot be emphasized often enough that we draw spiritual tests to ourself by the very intensity of our desire to know God and to be worthy of Him. While life itself is ever presenting opportunities for growth and development, we are not cognizant of this until the soul is quickened. When this happens we see clearly that every experience, every thought even, affords a chance to choose whom we will serve, God or mortal. Thus the challenges that come are not misfortunes but rare good fortune. In the end they bring us the peace for which we yearn. This has no connection with the insipid quiet of no-trial but is the tranquillity that envelopes us in spite of trial. Our human prayer for peace at any price contradicts the deeper prayer, "I shall be satisfied, when I awake, with thy likeness" (Psalms 17:15 A.V.).

Read Chapter 15. At this point another series of tests is in the offing. We are near the end of the road of human endeavor, and these will be the last ("I saw . . . seven angels with seven plagues, which are the last, for with them the wrath of God is ended"). Charles Fillmore's explanation of this is:

> An understanding of the "wrath" and the "plagues" . . . can be gained only by knowing the true character of God as principle—law—unalterable and unchangeable. When he keeps this law, man is blessed with the peace, the health, and the abundance of God, but if he tries to go contrary to the law he turns the power against himself and reaps the result in discord and inharmony. This adverse working of the law is termed the "anger" and the "wrath" and "the plagues" of God. Man is therefore the master of his own destiny, for he

has free will to choose whether or not he will work in harmony with divine law or against it.

We are determined to work in harmony with the Lord and have penetrated the disguise of the sense consciousness ("conquered the beast and its image"). Before meeting the oncoming tests we do exactly what we should do, turn to God. This always brings a realization of Him and our heart sings:

"Great and wonderful are thy deeds,
O Lord God the Almighty! . . .
For thou alone art holy."

Thus fortified we know that what is to come is spiritual in nature and will be beneficial (seven angels "robed in pure bright linen, and their breasts girded with golden girdles"). What the angels cause to come forth will not be easy to meet, yet we cannot abide in the sanctuary of God (temple), until our spiritual integrity is proved. No matter how frequently we retire to the secret place of the Most High, it is impossible to remain there until all imperfect states of consciousness are removed.

Contest between the spiritual and the sense self is now accelerated, for the time has come for the parting of their ways. We can continue no longer to have faith in Christ *and* the dragon. The latter is just exactly what Jesus said of the Devil: "He was a murderer from the beginning, and has nothing to do with the truth, because there is no truth in him" (John 8:44). Nevertheless, there are still many destructive phases of thought in us, those we have acquired through wrong thinking and those we have inherited from the race consciousness. It is exceedingly difficult to drive them out. We would like to ignore them, hoping they will depart of their own accord. This is vain wishing and even Jesus had to take a firm stand. "Begone, Satan!" (Matt. 4:10), was His command.

Read Chapter 16:1-11. With the pouring of the first four bowls, false beliefs regarding the body are attacked. Theoretically, we acknowledge the body to be pure spiritual substance, every cell permeated with the healing life of God. But can we sustain this when our body is afflicted? The first bowl inflicts "foul and evil sores"; the second and third make the sea and rivers become as blood; the fourth causes the sun to scorch as fire. These all symbolize unexpected calamities to our physical being. If our mortal self is in control we lay the blame on the Lord ("cursed the name of God who had power over these plagues"), and refuse to change our mind ("they did not repent and give him glory").

The same attitude persists when the fifth bowl is poured. It is aimed directly at the very center of the carnal mind ("the throne of the beast"). It is an amazing fact that we will endure all manner of distress rather than give up our habits of thought and action. We will seek help from every available earthly agency rather than turn to God and abide by His law. We want to change the condition but have great aversion to changing ourself. This shows the extent to which we are still in bondage to the satanic elements in us ("men . . . cursed the God of heaven for their pain and sores, and did not repent of their deeds").

Read Chapter 16:12-21. This section of the vision strikes at the belief in and love for the things of the world. These are extremely deep-seated and strong. In his unredeemed state man is much closer to the outer plane than he is to God and looks to it as the source of his good. He has faith in what he contacts with his five senses and what they report to him. This keeps his attention fixed on materiality as the only reality, and this has become so much of his thought that he is a slave to it. When his eyes are opened to the spiritual world he tries to follow Jesus' injunction, "Do not judge by appearance, but judge with right judgment" (John 7:24). This is not a simple thing to do, for he has his former convictions to contend with.

An attack on the belief in materiality begins as the sixth bowl is poured, which dries up the river Euphrates. This river supplied water to the ancient city of Babylon. Babylon was the capital of Babylonia, the land that was the enemy of Israel for centuries. The name *Babylon* was used repeatedly by the Old Testament prophets as a symbol of all that is unlike God, that is earthly power and wickedness in its most degraded form. It has the same significance here, and the belief it represents must be annihilated so that we may be prepared to receive our Lord ("prepare the way for the kings from the east").

Love for material things is a part of the carnal mind and when this mind is threatened, it makes a great effort to defend itself (the dragon, beast, and false prophet become very active). Unclean thoughts issue from it ("foul spirits like frogs" came out of the mouth of the dragon and his cohorts), and gather strength from kindred thoughts ("kings of the whole world"). The great day is approaching when the final battle between our human and divine self is to be waged, and fighting for its life the human rallies its forces ("they assembled them together at the place which is called in Hebrew Armageddon").

Near Megiddo (the older Hebrew form of Armageddon) was a famous battlefield of Israel. Here two decisive victories were won: Deborah and Barak defeated Sisera, King Jabin's general, (Judg. 5), and Gideon conquered the Midianites (Judg. 7). Here also Israel suffered two great defeats: King Saul was routed by the Philistines (I Sam. 31), and the good King Josiah was slain by Pharaoh Neco (II Kings 23). Armageddon literally means "mountain of Megiddo." The use of Armageddon is a clear indication that the approaching war is to take place on the heights, or is to be a battle between spiritual and satanic combatants.

We have seen the falseness of the sense consciousness revealed by the pouring of six bowls, and have taken the lessons to heart. Now we are ready for the seventh. When the angel pours his bowl into the air the Christ ("great voice came out of the temple, from the throne") announces the good news: "It is done!" The purification of our consciousness is continuing ("there were flashes of lightning, loud noises, peals of thunder"), but it is a shattering experience and our whole being quivers ("a great earthquake such as had never been since men were on the earth, so great was that earthquake"). We see more clearly than ever that we can serve mammon no longer for our belief in materialism has been violently shaken (Babylon is divided "and the cities of the nations fell"). Yet the remnant of the mortal self holds on and curses the Lord for the pain it is enduring ("cursed God for the plague").

This chapter is a turning point for the initiate. "It is done!"; that is, the tests which it has been so difficult for him to meet are now over. He sees evil for what it is, an accumulation of erroneous beliefs in his own consciousness. He realizes that there is no outer power opposing him, nothing to deter his onward march except himself. And though he has not fully conquered his inner foes, from now on the remaining ones are displayed clearly. He is able to view them in a more detached frame of mind and is finally able to let his Christ cast them out.

Read Chapter 17:1-6. Our angel self now reveals the depravity of sensuousness which is represented by the great harlot. The feminine stands for the feeling nature, in which lustful desires arise, and they have enticed us to sense indulgence ("with the wine of whose fornication the dwellers on earth have become drunk"). Sensuality is an integral part of both materialism (Babylon) and the carnal nature (dragon); the vision is of "a woman sitting on a scarlet beast which was full of blasphemous names, and it had seven heads and ten horns."

Outwardly, lust appears to be attractive and desirable ("the woman was arrayed in purple and scarlet, and bedecked with gold and jewels and pearls"), but its repulsiveness cannot be hidden (she holds in her hand "a golden cup full of abominations and the impurities of her fornication"). Her name is "Babylon the great, mother of harlots and of earth's abominations." It is unbridled sensuality that saps our life force (she was "drunk with the blood of the saints").

At first glance we are uncertain of the meaning of this ("when I saw her I marveled greatly").

Read Chapter 17:7-18. An answer to our query is promptly given ("I will tell you the mystery of the woman, and of the beast with seven heads and ten horns that carried her"). All forms of sin spring from the lower nature (beast), and end in ruin ("the beast that you saw was, and is not, and is to ascend from the bottomless pit and go to perdition"). This is puzzling to mortal thought ("the dwellers on earth . . . will marvel"), but Spirit ("this calls for a mind with wisdom") knows the beginning and end of iniquity.

The explanation given of the seven heads and ten horns of the beast is rather ambiguous. The seven heads are "seven hills" and also "seven kings." Rome was built on seven hills and its rulers had controlled a large portion of the earth for many years (five kings "have fallen"), and still have power ("one is"). Its dominion will last for a time ("the other has not yet come, and when he comes he must remain only a little while"). The ten horns are ten kings who "gave over their power and authority to the beast," but Rome is bound for destruction. The persecuted Christians of the period would understand and be heartened by this prediction.

Spiritually interpreted, this is a prophecy that the materialism which Rome, like Babylon, represents is doomed to perish. Our worldly beliefs vie with our righteous thoughts ("make war on the Lamb"), but they shall be worsted in the struggle ("the Lamb will conquer them, for he is Lord of lords, and King of kings").

Here a most important point is brought to light. Evil is self-destructive. The ignoble elements in the sense consciousness are always at war with one another ("the ten horns that you saw, they and the beast will hate the harlot; they will . . . burn her up with fire"). With all its seeming power, iniquity can endure only until we rise above it in consciousness ("until the words of God shall be fulfilled"). The cardinal sin is rejection of Him; within the sin is the seed of its own demise. "Though the mills of God grind slowly, yet they grind exceeding small."

Read Chapter 18. We come now to the fulfillment of the prophecy of Chapter 14:8, "Fallen, fallen, is Babylon the great." "Coming events cast their shadows before," for all outer conditions are the outpicturing of thought. When this is centered on materiality (Babylon), our feeling nature also becomes attached to them and the whole self is involved in error. This is a perversion of the greatest gift God gave us, love, and such sets into operation a chain of events that lead to devastation. "You shall love the Lord your God with all your heart, and with all your soul, and with all your mind" (Matt. 22:37). Love for Him is the highest use to which the faculty can be put. As we become aware of His love for us, a compassion that endures despite our ignorance and indifference, we withdraw our affection from the world and let it flow in a mighty stream to Him. Then we are automatically free from an attachment to all that Babylon represents, and for us it has indeed "fallen."

This chapter is reminiscent of the songs of doom in Isaiah 13, 14, 34, and Jeremiah 50, 51, against Babylon. The language is poetic, and in a spiritual sense it relates the many realizations that come to mind regarding the futility of giving our loyalty and devotion to earthly things. Our higher consciousness rends the veil that we may see how utterly devoid they are of the good we attributed to them. The revelation is in three parts.

The first angel ("having great authority") assures us that our mistaken belief in the desirability of the material realm is passing away ("Fallen, fallen is Babylon the great . . . a dwelling place of demons, . . . haunt of every foul spirit").

The second angel ("voice from heaven") announces that the moment has arrived to detach ourself completely from all that Babylon stands for and

save ourself from harm ("Come out of her . . . lest
you take part in her sins . . . share in her plagues").
In the past we had often entertained the suspicion
that physical law was above God's law; now we know
the latter is supreme ("so shall her plagues come in a
single day," and pestilence, mourning, and famine
will result; "she shall be burned with fire," for
"mighty is the Lord God who judges her"). Even the
outer benefits we attributed to the world are no
more ("the merchants of the earth weep and mourn
for her, since no one buys their cargo any more").
The beautiful objects that gave us an aesthetic pleasure but which we associated with materiality have
disappeared ("all thy dainties and thy splendor are
lost to thee"). Momentarily, our human emotions
cry out "as they saw the smoke of her burning," but
our spiritual self rejoices that our belief in a life apart
from Spirit has come to an end. This judgment is
confirmed by Him ("God has given judgment for
you against her!").

The third angel ("mighty angel") shows us that all
joy has departed from what we once thought could
furnish happiness ("the sound of harpers and min-
strels, of flute players and trumpeters" is "heard in
thee no more . . . and the voice of bridegroom and
bride"). All prosperity based on worldly ambition
has vanished ("a craftsmen of any craft shall be
found in thee no more . . . the sound of the mill-
stone shall be heard in thee no more"). Once the
misconception that our best interests lie in the outer
was strong enough to overpower our faith in God as

the giver of every good and perfect gift ("in her was found the blood of prophets and of saints"), but this too has been dissolved.

> "So shall Babylon the great city be thrown down with violence,
> and shall be found no more."

The New Birth

Revelation 19–22

During the previous five visions the initiate has become increasingly aware of the falsity of the sense consciousness and has realized that his indwelling Christ has shown him how to separate the true from the untrue. As inner light dispels the darkness of mortal thought we move rapidly toward the complete giving of ourself to God. "Father, into thy hands I commit my spirit!" were Jesus' words that precipitated the Resurrection. All struggle is coming to an end for we know that the battle is not ours but His.

This chapter covers the sixth and seventh visions. With the sixth we are on the threshold of victory. The seventh is a vision of that perfection and peace which is ours when we have made the mighty overcomings that allow the divine self to come forth.

"I have loved you with an everlasting love;
therefore I have continued my faithfulness to you"

(Jer. 31:3).

Because of God's love He is ever drawing us. We took His hand as we walked through the dark forests and muddy rivers of sense, and we shall arrive safely on that beautiful shore He prepared for every soul.

Sixth Vision—Victory of the Word of God

Revelation 19—20

Read Chapter 19:1-10. At last we are free from the belief in materiality, and there is no joy equal to that which wells up in our heart when we understand that God is all. "Hallelujah! Salvation and glory, and power belong to our God." All the spiritual forces of our being (the twenty- four elders, four living creatures, and "the voice of a great multitude") join in praise to Him. We shout in ecstasy for "the Lord, our God the Almighty reigns."

This elevation in consciousness brings the realization that our soul is to be united with its Christ ("the marriage of the Lamb has come . . . his Bride has made herself ready"). The soul is our self-consciousness, our awareness of ourself as an individual. The Lamb is the spiritual self, the Christ indwelling. Through aspiration to be one with Christ our soul is gradually made ready. We learn to look to the divine only, we learn to dispel the destructive thoughts and feelings that have generated through eons of time. When at last our soul takes on the pristine purity it had when the Lord God breathed into it the breath of life, we know that the time is ripe for human identity to be merged with spiritual identity. Marriage with the Christ is ready to be consummated.

Read Chapter 19:11-21. This is our second encounter with the rider of the white horse who appeared when the first seal was opened (6:2), and

was revealed as the Christ. Due to our fuller understanding, we know that He is called "Faithful and
True," and the description of Him uses the Christ
symbols ("his eyes are like a flame of fire, and on his
head are many diadems"). His mission is to defend
justice and contend against evil ("in righteousness he
judges and makes war"). His name is called "The
Word of God."

Up to this point we have done much work in our
own consciousness by using the divine Word, and
this was necessary. The time has come for us to realize that victory is to be gained not by what *we* can do
even with God's help, but by what we can let the
Christ do through us. Our great teachers knew the
limitations of self-effort. Moses said to the Children
of Israel, "The LORD will fight for you, and you
have only to be still" (Exod. 14:14). Jesus said, "The
Father who dwells in me does his works"(John
14:10). Now we too can "let go and let God."

As we trust Christ fully, He assumes complete
charge. He has infinite resources to call upon ("the
armies of heaven"), and is equipped for the task at
hand ("from his mouth issues a sharp sword . . . and
he will rule them with a rod of iron"). He carries the
designation of divine power and authority ("King of
kings and Lord of lords"). The devastation of the
enemies of the Lord, the carnal self, is to be complete (an angel summons even "the birds that fly in
midheaven" to gather for "the great supper of God,
to eat the flesh of kings . . . and the flesh of mighty
men").

The hosts of the mortal self ("the beast and the kings of the earth with their armies," and the false prophet) join to wage war against Christ and His hosts. This is the great battle of Armageddon, the climactic inner conflict between our spiritual consciousness and the carnal mind, between faith in God and belief in the power of the material world. Our confidence in Him is complete, and the battle is soon over. False beliefs are powerless against the might of Christ and are quickly vanquished (beast and false prophet "were thrown alive into the lake of fire that burns with brimstone"). The phrase "lake of fire" is used in various apocalyptic writings to denote total destruction. Here it means that that portion of the total error belief symbolized by the beast and false prophet has been annihilated.

Read Chapter 20:1-6. There still remains the very crux of the carnal mind to be dealt with (dragon). As part of this has been overthrown (the two beasts destroyed), its activity is greatly restricted. Our spiritual self ("an angel coming down from heaven") is able to hold the carnal mind captive for a lengthy period ("he seized the dragon, that ancient serpent, who is the Devil and Satan, and bound him for a thousand years"). The phrase "a thousand years" as used here refers to an indefinite time during which our spiritual consciousness is strong enough to restrain the carnal mind. We realize, however, that it will again assert itself ("he [dragon] must be loosed for a little while").

Relieved of pressure from sense thoughts, we see clearly that divine justice is always functioning ("I saw thrones, and seated on them were those [the saints] to whom judgment was committed"). Sometimes it has seemed that loyalty to spiritual ideals puts us at a disadvantage in dealing with those in personal consciousness ("beheaded for their testimony to Jesus, and for the word of God"). Now we see that the reward is great for the soul that has refused to lend itself to iniquity ("had not worshiped the beast"), for we have a spiritual companionship that entitles us to commune with Him ("reigned with Christ a thousand years").

The "thousand years" here refers to the millennium, or thousand years when Christ reigns. It was a popular expression in apocalyptic writings, and denotes an interval of peace for the faithful, not an actual time. In our own experience, the millennium refers to that stage in our ongoing that is marked by a sense of inward serenity and the outer manifestation of blessings. It does not imply that the mortal self has been fully conquered, but only held in abeyance. In the several years of His ministry, Jesus expressed good to the fullest. He was master of Himself and the conditions about Him, but it was not until the Resurrection that all which belonged to the human state He had assumed was completely overcome. At the beginning of our spiritual climb we are conscious of our Lord on many occasions, yet we drop back to mortal thinking within a short time—running in and out of heaven, as it were. Now we have gained a more sustained realization of Christ; we feel His peace more often and for longer periods.

"This is the first resurrection." It is a holy and blessed state ("they shall be priests of God and of Christ"), and liberates us from the "second death." An explanation of the second death will be given when the term is used again in the latter part of this chapter.

Read Chapter 20:7-15. Eventually the complete spiritualizing of the soul is to be accomplished. Our time of resting in the Lord comes to an end ("when the thousand years are ended"), and we must deal once more with the carnal mind ("Satan will be loosed from his prison"). The great deceiver strikes again, rallying a formidable army, this time represented by Gog and Magog. In the book of Ezekiel, from which these names were taken, the prophet calls Gog the chief prince of Meshech and Tubal, from the land of Magog, an imaginary character and place. Gog is pictured as leading a large nation from the north, Magog, against Israel. Ezekiel prophesied the restoration of Israel but said that Gog of the country of Magog would attempt to keep the restoration from taking place. The names are used symbolically in Revelation also and represent malicious forces that attack the spiritual. Charles Fillmore says that Gog and Magog signify:

> The satanic or selfish thought force in human consciousness, warring against the true thought force that is based upon the ideas taught and demonstrated by Jesus Christ.

Unity of purpose and effort is becoming widely
recognized as the most potent means to attain any
desired end. . . . Sense wisdom is often resistant, however; the law of love is not observed. There arise antagonism, combativeness, war. What turmoil will result in
this battle royal between the organized forces of man
thought in the earth no one can tell. It is the battle of
Gog and Magog, which will end only when the satanic
or selfish thought is cast out of human consciousness.
The push and the pull of these two forces are sure for a
time to produce discord in the affairs of men. Those
who are not organized against it will suffer—they will
be ground between the millstones of material conditions unless they know how to rise above them.

But there is another organized thought force. It is
based upon the ideas promulgated by Jesus Christ. It
believes in love, reason, honesty, justice, unselfishness,
nonresistance, and, above all, in the guidance and wisdom and power of a Mind that is higher than that of the
present race consciousness. This organized thought of
spiritual-minded men and women will, through the
ideas planted in the race thought by Jesus Christ, make
unity with Divine Mind and establish right here in earth
conditions of peace and harmony. It will not be accomplished by an outside deity, but by inner forces' acting
through the souls of those dwelling on earth (MD 239).

In the ensuing conflict the hosts of Satan are numerous ("like the sand of the sea"), but once again we
behold the miracle-working power of Christ ("fire
came down from heaven and consumed them"). The
carnal self (Satan, Gog, and Magog) is utterly defeated ("thrown into the lake of fire and brimstone
where the beast and the false prophet were").

"And they will be tormented day and night for
ever and ever." This dire fate befalls the conscious-

ness that entertains the belief in separation from God, the good. Evil thoughts form evil conditions which cause torment. Jesus said, "You, therefore, must be perfect, as your heavenly Father is perfect" (Matt. 5:48). Our well-being is in exact ratio to our compliance with this standard of righteousness. Through faith in and obedience to the Christ, all carnality is completely eradicated and no longer has any hold whatever on our soul.

Again we perceive the majesty and power of God ("I saw a great white throne and him who sat upon it"). A similar vision came to us at the beginning of our definite work in consciousness and spurred us on. Now our work is done, the ideal has become real. Once more we stand before our Maker to be judged.

> And I saw the dead, great and small, standing before the throne, and books were opened. Also another book was opened, which is the book of life. And the dead were judged by what was written in the books, by what they had done (Rev. 20:12).

This verse has given rise to the doctrine of Judgment Day, which has struck terror to the hearts of men. In Truth we do not subscribe to the belief that there is a final judgment after physical death. Charles Fillmore says, "The 'day of judgment' to us is any day that we get the fruit in body and affairs of some thought or word that we have expressed" (JC 161). Cause and effect operate throughout the eternal existence of the soul. For our righteous thoughts the law gives harmony throughout our being; for our negative thoughts the just law brings dissension and limitation. All are judged according to their works.

A literal interpretation of these sentences has also filled men with fear of God: "Then Death and Hades were thrown into the lake of fire. This is the second death, the lake of fire." In Truth we hold the meaning to be that so long as we are governed by a consciousness that denies the omnipresence of Good, we suffer the tortures of the damned. Faith in sin, sickness, and lack results in the absence of life. Death has never been a part of the divine plan. As Paul says, "To set the mind on the flesh is death, but to set the mind on the Spirit is life and peace" (Rom. 8:6). When false beliefs are cleansed from consciousness we enter into the more abundant life of Christ.

According to the general theological teaching, the first death is the dissolution of the physical body and the second death is the consignment of sinners to an everlasting Hell. Charles Fillmore gives a metaphysical interpretation of the two deaths:

> Adam, as originally created, was in illumination. Spirit continually breathed into him the inspiration and knowledge that gave him superior understanding. But he began eating (or appropriating) ideas of two powers—God and not-God, good and evil. The result, so the allegory relates, was a falling away from life and all that it involves. This was the first death.
>
> Men do not think of the first death in its relation to the second death. The latter enters when the soul loses control of the body, when the functional activities cease and the physical organism dissolves. . . . Sinners (men who believe in two powers, good and evil) are already dead. They do not have to wait until the body

> stops acting, to know the conditions that prevail in death. . . . The first death is death of the light and the life of Spirit in our consciousness, and the result is a withdrawal of the soul from the organism (TT 146, 147).

Overcoming the first and second death is of vital importance to those who would follow Jesus Christ all the way. As the soul is spiritualized so is the body, until it becomes like the resurrected body of Jesus Christ. Paul refers to physical death as the last enemy to be abolished and says, "For as in Adam all die, so also in Christ shall all be made alive" (I Cor. 15:22). Jesus declared, "I am the resurrection and the life . . . and whoever lives and believes in me shall never die" (John 11:25, 26). In Truth we accept His words literally:

> The whole secret of the demonstration of Christ is that we shall come to realize our original sinlessness. Sin and the consciousness of sin are the cause of all darkness and death. No amount of physical health can overcome the sins of the carnal mind. Unless he is regenerated under the Jesus Christ teaching, man is a whited sepulcher, "full of dead men's bones." So you are not really alive, wholly alive, safely alive, eternally alive, until you get right where Jesus Christ was and is. He cultivated and demonstrated those thoughts which are the foundation of mental harmony, and if we study His life we shall see just how we must follow Him into His life, become part of it, and live in eternal life, here and now (TT 154, 155).

By means of these remarkable visions our indwelling Christ has shown us that the only real world is that which God created. Evil has no power except what we give it by acknowledgment and faith. Christ has been with us throughout our struggles to overcome this adverse consciousness and the triumph is His. Through our surrender to God, He has repossessed the soul to which He gave life in that dim and distant past "when the morning stars sang together," when "all the sons of God shouted for joy" (Job 38:7). We realize now that Christ is the way, the truth, and the life, and that our being is actually "hid with Christ in God." This awareness produces the beatific seventh vision.

Seventh Vision — the New Heaven and the New Earth

Revelation 21, 22

For even the most advanced soul, this vision reveals a state of consciousness yet to be attained. Only Jesus Christ has proved himself worthy to be called the Son of God in expression, though every soul has buried deep within it the pattern of divinity. Through the ages a few individuals have so merged themselves with God that they have been as lights along the way for every initiate. As we "are citizens of Heaven" (Phil. 3:20 N.E.B.), we cannot avoid our destiny, and it is a crucial moment in our life when we undertake the difficult task of soul unfoldment. Revelation relates this in detail, and the last two chapters tell what is in store for us when we shall have overcome all that is unlike God and are established in the light of His all-pervading love. These chapters consist of a series of realizations pouring from the redeemed consciousness.

"Behold, I make all things new" is the theme of the final vision. It presents the view of a transformed world resulting from a transformed consciousness. It is the answer to our prayer, "Thy kingdom come . . . On earth as it is in heaven." The initiate has finished the course laid out for him by Jesus Christ, and henceforth he lives in the world of spiritual reality.

The work of redemption begins with a *revelation* of spiritual man, the Christ, the Son of God, as given in the first chapter of the book. It ends with a *realization* of Christ as our only life and the means by which we express the powers God implanted within us. A perfect world has always existed; now we can accept the invitation to enter it: "Come, O blessed of my Father, inherit the kingdom prepared for you from the foundation of the world" (Matt. 25:34). We have reached the end of the quest, the goal of man's high calling. We have fulfilled our divine destiny as perceived by Isaiah:

"By myself I have sworn,
    from my mouth has gone forth in righteousness
    a word that shall not return:
'To me every knee shall bow,
    every tongue shall swear' "

(Isa. 45:23).

The number *twelve,* representing perfection, is used throughout the vision. It denotes the full spiritual realization that comes when permanent union is made with the Christ.

Of the New Jerusalem, Charles Fillmore says:

> This state (glory of God) comes into our consciousness just as fast as we will let it by overcoming the "abominations and lies" of materiality. People all over this earth are today coming into this "New Jerusalem" which is let down out of heaven. They are being renovated and purified by an inner life current entering their bodies through their mind, and they can testify that this new heaven and new earth is not an illusion but a veritable fact. They feel the new life quickening the nerve centers. The Principle of Life is so conscious that they realize that the divine relation between Father and son is established (Unity).

Read Chapter 21:1-8. The majestic words, "And God saw everything that he had made, and behold, it was very good" (Gen. 1:31), are now fulfilled. His good is not something apart from us but something in which we live, move, and have being. With a new and vitalized consciousness we perceive the inner and outer realms as they are in Spirit ("a new heaven and a new earth"). Our human conception of them has gone ("the first heaven and the first earth had passed away, and the sea was no more"). The sea represents "a type of the race thought which has formed itself into vibratory waves of ignorance, in which people swim and eat and fight and die as fishes in the sea" (Unity). In spiritual consciousness, ignorance of God has ceased to be.

The holiness or wholeness of the Almighty ("new Jerusalem, coming down out of heaven from God") is as beautiful as "a bride adorned for her husband." Our belief that the kingdom of God is within, and that He will neither leave nor forsake us, is verified ("Behold, the dwelling of God is with men. He will dwell with them, and they shall be his people, and God himself will be with them"). He frees us from those troubles that beset the mortal: sorrow, death, and pain ("he will wipe away every tear from their eyes, and death shall be no more, neither shall there be mourning nor crying nor pain"). All things are in a constant state of renewal, for God is both the beginning and end of life ("I am the Alpha and the Omega"). He gives of His inspiration to all who seek it ("To the thirsty I will give . . . from the fountain of the water of life").

In each of the letters to the seven churches (Rev. 3, 4), a promise is made to "him who conquers." We understand now that the only overcoming to be made is the belief in separation from God; the only attainment to be reached is the realization, "I and the Father are one" (John 10:30). The final promise given here covers the seven previous ones and unites them: "He who conquers shall have this heritage, and I will be his God, and he shall be my son."

There is no place in the perfected consciousness for the destructive and savage thoughts that infest the sense mind ("their lot shall be in the lake that burns with fire and brimstone").

Read Chapter 21:9-27. These verses describe in

vivid and colorful words the beauty and harmony of
the spiritual realm of which we have now become
aware. At the start of our search for God we had
little conception of what His world is like. Our idea
was vague and as imperfect as our own soul. Now
that we have attained a high level of development, a
mental picture of the ideal state becomes crystal
clear, "having the glory of God," and we perceive it
in detail.

Everything about the spiritualized consciousness
(holy city) is in exact proportion. The number
twelve as used here symbolizes the twelve faculties
of man. When these are spiritually developed they
become the cornerstones of divine realization
(twelve gates in the wall around the city, twelve
angels at the gates and upon the gates the names of
the twelve tribes of Israel, twelve foundations bearing the names of the Twelve Apostles). Perfect balance is maintained for "the city lies foursquare, its
length the same as its breadth." The square was the
symbol of perfection to the Greeks; to the Jews *foursquare* meant the cube which was the shape of the
Holy of Holies in their Temple; to the Christians,
who were both Gentile and Jew, it meant the perfected life of Jesus Christ. To the spiritual aspirant
foursquare signifies that firm and solid foundation
of absolute truth upon which the divine man ever
stands. The loveliness of the New Jerusalem is
enhanced by the twelve precious stones which adorn
it and by the pure gold of its streets.

It is important to remember that these symbols are used not to describe an actual place, but to convey the idea that when we function in spiritual consciousness our inner world becomes substantial, orderly, and beautiful. Then these qualities cannot but be reflected in our outer world also.

No longer are we dependent upon physical supports of any kind. There is no need for a place in which to worship God, for true worship takes place in the inner sanctuary of our own being ("I saw no temple in the city, for its temple is the Lord God the Almighty and the Lamb"). The light that illumines the soul is not that afforded by sun and moon, but shines directly from the indwelling Spirit ("the city has no need of sun or moon to shine upon it, for the glory of God is its light, and its lamp is the Lamb"). Spiritual consciousness, being God-given, is available to all ("its gates shall never be shut"), yet only those who are worthy (whose names are "written in the Lamb's book of life") can abide therein.

Read Chapter 22:1-5. The symbols used remind us of Eden, with its river that watered the Garden and the tree of life (Gen. 2). In the allegory the river branched into four parts; now it flows in a steady stream from the Godhead and becomes the "river of the water of life." As such it represents the inspiration of the Holy Spirit, which alone can quench the thirst of the soul. Jesus said, "Whoever drinks of the water that I shall give him will never thirst; the water that I shall give him will become in him a spring of water welling up to eternal life" (John 4:14).

On "either side of the river" is the tree of life. The Eden account relates that the Lord God gave man (Adam) permission to eat of this tree, but when he chose to eat instead of the tree of the knowledge of good and evil, the cherubim with a flaming sword guarded the tree of life. Man in a sinning state cannot partake of it:

> The "tree of life" is the inherent life of the organism; it is symbolized in the physical by the nerves and the spinal column. The spinal column represents the tree; the nerves, which carry the living waters, are the branches and leaves of the tree. Every month a transmutation of the living waters takes place, under divine order; thus are the "twelve *manner* of fruits" produced by the "tree of life . . . in the midst of the garden," the spiritualized body. . . . Man is kept from partaking of this precious, healing, life-giving fruit only by thoughts of sensuality. When this phase of sense consciousness is taken up in Truth and eliminated, and the idea of purity is built in, man's body begins to express its original holiness and perfection. We eat of the fruit of the "tree of life" when we appropriate ideas of divine life, ceasing to dwell on life as something that comes and goes, or something that is governed by birth and death (MD 664).

In the redeemed consciousness we share in the sustaining life of God ("the leaves of the tree were for the healing of the nations"), and our body is restored. The age-old promise is fulfilled, "But for you who fear my name the sun of righteousness shall rise, with healing in its wings" (Mal. 4:2).

All struggle is now over and nothing shall again mar the soul ("there shall no more be anything accursed"). God is in full control, a living presence ("the throne of God and of the Lamb shall be in it"). We shall be with Him and serve Him. His light has scattered the darkness. We have asserted the dominion He gave us and "shall reign for ever and ever."

Read Chapter 22:6-21. These verses constitute an epilogue, consisting of seven admonitions and a benediction. In the prologue, seven messages were addressed to the initiate pointing out deficiencies in consciousness to be overcome in order that he might proceed on his spiritual journey. In the epilogue an equal number of admonitions are addressed to him, recommending procedures to be followed so that he may retain the spiritual development he has won. The emphasis is upon the necessity for keeping the words of Jesus Christ which are revealed in this book.

> 1. "And behold, I am coming soon." Blessed is he who keeps the words of the prophecy of this book (22:7).

The declaration, "I am coming soon," is repeated three times in the admonitions, each time with a different shade of meaning but all for the purpose of calling attention to the prompt action of Spirit. In this case, the assurance is given that He answers our call swiftly when we are deserving of His aid. We are blessed when we keep "the words of the prophecy of this book." The last of the judges, Samuel, reminded his people, "To obey is better than sacrifice . . . to hearken than the fat of rams" (I Sam. 15:22). Having advanced spiritually, we can exclaim with the Psalmist,

"I delight to do thy will, O my God;
thy law is within my heart"

(Psalms 40:8).

Joyful and loving obedience brings His immediate response, and induces the hallowed or holy state which "blessed" means in a spiritual sense.

> 2. I John am he who heard and saw these things. And when I heard and saw them, I fell down to worship at the feet of the angel who showed them to me; but he said to me, "You must not do that! I am a fellow servant with you and your brethren the prophets, and with those who keep the words of this book. Worship God" (22:8, 9).

As we behold the splendor of the spiritual realm we may think it is our own illumined consciousness (angel) that has revealed it, and thus fall into self-adulation and spiritual pride. The warning is to keep in mind that God is the source of light and life. Jesus, the perfect man, said, "Why callest thou me good? *there is* none good but one, *that is,* God" (Matt. 19:17 A.V.). Also He said, "The Father is greater than I" (John 14:28). We are to worship God only.

> 3. And he said to me, "Do not seal up the words of the prophecy of this book, for the time is near. Let the evildoer still do evil, and the filthy still be filthy, and the righteous still do right, and the holy still be holy."

> "Behold, I am coming soon, bringing my recompense, to repay everyone for what he has done...."
>
> Blessed are those who wash their robes, that they may have the right to the tree of life and that they may enter the city by the gates. Outside are the dogs and sorcerers ... and every one who loves and practices falsehood (22:10-15).

We are not to keep His word secret, but to declare it. His message of salvation is for all ("Do not seal up the words of the prophecy of this book"). Yet we should not attempt to coerce anyone, for each soul has a God-given right to freedom of choice ("the righteous still do right, and the holy still be holy"). Here the promise, "I am coming soon," applies to the divine law of compensation, giving what is deserved ("repay every one for what he has done"). Those who cleanse themselves of carnality ("wash their robes") earn the right to partake of the pure life of Spirit ("have the right to the tree of life") and live with Christ ("enter the city by the gates"). Those who allow sense consciousness to govern them ("every one who loves and practices falsehood") are denied this privilege.

> 4. "I Jesus have sent my angel to you with this testimony for the churches. I am the root and the offspring of David, the bright morning star" (22:16).

Jesus' mission was to show us the Father and reveal the way to Him. As our beloved teacher and healer He is ever with us to guide, encourage, and uphold. He makes himself known ("sent my angel"), and testifies to the truth. Jesus is the Anointed One, the Messiah ("the root and the offspring of David"), and shines in our life as the bright, the morning star.

5. The Spirit and the Bride say, "Come." And let him who hears say, "Come." And let him who is thirsty come, let him who desires take the water of life without price (22:17).

Our Lord's invitation to come to Him runs like a mighty refrain throughout the Bible. Isaiah sums it up in the words,

"Incline your ear, and come unto me;
    hear, that your soul may live"

(Isa. 55:3).

Jesus adds to it, "Come to me, all who labor and are heavy laden, and I will give you rest" (Matt. 11:28). Here we are urged again to "come." Spirit says it; our ears are attuned to Him and we repeat it; and at times of thirsting for the inspiration of Spirit, we are reminded to come and drink freely of the "water of life."

6. I warn every one who hears the words of the prophecy of this book: if any one adds to them, God will add to him the plagues described in this book, and if any one takes away from the words of the book of this prophecy, God will take away his share in the tree of life and in the holy city, which are described in this book (22:18, 19).

The pattern of spiritual unfoldment laid out in Revelation is full and complete. Nothing is to be added, nothing taken away. It is the only way for those who are desirous of following Jesus Christ into the kingdom of heaven.

There are some who would add to the concise and straightforward directions given by Him through these visions. Intricate mysteries and secret initiations, elaborate rituals and ceremonies offer to show the way. Our spiritual development does not come through these. It results from turning again and again to Christ, the one and only reliable guide, and being obedient to His words.

There are others who promise a shortcut to the kingdom and would dispense with the daily overcomings that are part of the discipline of the soul. There are no shortcuts. Every inch of the path must be traversed. After we have started our conscious spiritual unfoldment there are periods when we feel close to Him and progress rapidly. At other times we seem to be separated from Him and, like Job, cry out in pain and discouragement:

"Oh, that I knew where I might find him . . .
Behold, I go forward, but he is not there;
     and backward, but I cannot perceive him"
                                        (Job 23:3-8).

Apart from Him and unable to break the chain of mortal thought that enslaves us, we may remain at a certain level of spiritual development for many years, even for the remainder of an incarnation. Eventually, however, the prodigal returns to the Father's house. We are with our Lord once more and the practice of the presence of God becomes the natural way of living. On we go with our hand in His, to enter into a higher cycle of unfoldment.

As we take each forward step there is a test to be passed before we stand firmly on higher ground. "Put me to the test, says the Lord" (Mal. 3:10), and prove Him we can and do. The one impossibility is to change one iota of God's law, but in changing ourself we "put on the new nature, created after the likeness of God in true righteousness and holiness" (Eph. 4:24).

> 7. He who testifies to these things says, "Surely I am coming soon." Amen. Come, Lord Jesus! (22:20)

Jesus Christ is the One who testifies that the revelation of God as given by Him in this book is wholly true. During His earthly ministry Jesus said, "Which is the greater . . . Is it not the one who sits at table? But I am among you as one who serves" (Luke 22:27), and also, "Lo, I am with you always, to the close of the age" (Matt. 28:20). Now for the third time and in this final admonition John (speaking for Jesus) verifies the great and wonderful truth that He is always near. To give special emphasis the word *surely* prefaces "I am coming soon." Amen, so be it. The battle over self is won and we respond, " 'Come, Lord Jesus!' Come to share with us your love and wisdom, come to be our guide and our redeemer."

Revelation ends with the benediction, "The grace

of the Lord Jesus be with all the saints. Amen." The word *saints* has been used repeatedly to mean those who acknowledge and are faithful to Him. "Follow me" is His instruction. This book is our assurance that following Him leads to the very apex of spiritual attainment and brings the deep and abiding realization:

"Lord, thou hast been our dwelling place
in all generations.
Before the mountains were brought forth,
or ever thou hadst formed the earth and the
world,
from everlasting to everlasting thou art God"
(Psalms 90:1, 2).

PRINTED U.S.A.   103F-2713-5M-4-78